Lecture Notes in Computer Science 15424

Founding Editors

Gerhard Goos
Juris Hartmanis

The series Lecture Notes in Computer Science (LNCS), including its subseries Lecture Notes in Artificial Intelligence (LNAI) and Lecture Notes in Bioinformatics (LNBI), has established itself as a medium for the publication of new developments in computer science and information technology research, teaching, and education.

LNCS enjoys close cooperation with the computer science R & D community, the series counts many renowned academics among its volume editors and paper authors, and collaborates with prestigious societies. Its mission is to serve this international community by providing an invaluable service, mainly focused on the publication of conference and workshop proceedings and postproceedings. LNCS commenced publication in 1973.

Jing Zeng · Liang-Jie Zhang
Editors

Edge Computing – EDGE 2024

8th International Conference
Held as Part of the Services Conference Federation, SCF 2024
Bangkok, Thailand, November 16–19, 2024
Proceedings

 Springer

Editors
Jing Zeng
China Gridcom Co., Ltd.
Shenzhen, China

Liang-Jie Zhang 🆔
Shenzhen University
Shenzhen, China

ISSN 0302-9743   ISSN 1611-3349 (electronic)
Lecture Notes in Computer Science
ISBN 978-3-031-77068-5   ISBN 978-3-031-77069-2 (eBook)
https://doi.org/10.1007/978-3-031-77069-2

Preface

The 2024 International Congress on Edge Computing (EDGE 2024) aimed to provide an international forum to formally explore various business insights into all kinds of value-added "services". Edge Computing is a key enabler in exploring business insights and economics of services.

EDGE 2024 was a member of the Services Conference Federation (SCF). SCF 2024 had the following 10 collocated service-oriented sister conferences: 2024 International Conference on Services Computing (SCC 2024), 2024 International Conference on Big Data (BigData 2024), 2024 International Conference on AI and Multmodal Services (AIMS 2024), 2024 International Conference on Metaverse (Metaverse 2024), 2024 International Conference on Internet of Things (ICIOT 2024), 2024 International Conference on Cognitive Computing (ICCC 2024), 2024 International Conference on Edge Computing (EDGE 2024), 2024 International Conference on Blockchain (ICBC 2024), 2024 International Conference on Cloud Computing (CLOUD 2024), and 2024 International Conference on Web Services (ICWS 2024).

As the founding member of the Services Conference Federation (SCF), the first **International Conference on Web Services (ICWS)** was held in June 2003 in Las Vegas, USA. Meanwhile, the First International Conference on Web Services - Europe 2003 (ICWS-Europe 2003) was held in Germany in October 2003. ICWS-Europe 2003 was an extended event of the 2003 International Conference on Web Services (ICWS 2003) in Europe. In 2004, ICWS-Europe was changed to the European Conference on Web Services (ECOWS), which was held at Erfurt, Germany. Sponsored by the Services Society and Springer, SCF 2018 and SCF 2019 were held successfully in Seattle and San Diego, USA. SCF 2020 and SCF 2021 were held successfully online and in Shenzhen, China. To celebrate its 21st birthday, SCF 2024 was held on November 16–19, 2024, in Bangkok, Thailand.

This volume presents the accepted papers of EDGE 2024, held in Bangkok as an onsite conference during November 16–19 2024. EDGE 2024's major topics included but were not limited to: Edge Storage, Edge Connections, Edge Analytics, Edge AI, Edge Processing Engine, Industry-Specific Edges, Edge Application Innovations, 5G and Edge, 5G and Cloud, AIGC for Edge.

EDGE 2024 received 16 submissions, and accepted 8 papers. Each was reviewed and selected by at least three independent members of the EDGE 2024 International Program Committee in a single-blind review process. We are pleased to thank the authors whose submissions and participation made this conference possible. We also want to express our thanks to the Organizing Committee and Program Committee members, for their dedication in helping to organize the conference and reviewing the submissions. We look forward to your great contributions as volunteers, authors, and conference participants in the fast-growing worldwide services innovations community.

November 2024   Jing Zeng
Liang-Jie Zhang

Organization

General Chair

Chunpeng Ge   Shandong University, China

Program Chair

Jing Zeng   China Gridcom Co., Ltd., China

Services Conference Federation (SCF 2024)

General Chairs

Ali Arsanjani   Google Cloud, USA
Wu Chou   Essenlix Corporation, USA

Coordinating Program Chair

Liang-Jie Zhang   Shenzhen University, China

CFO and International Affairs Chair

Min Luo   Georgia Tech, USA

Operation Committee

Jing Zeng   China Gridcom Co., Ltd., China
Yishuang Ning   Tsinghua University, China
Sheng He   Tsinghua University, China
Zhuolin Mei   Jiujiang University, China

Steering Committee

Calton Pu (Co-chair)   Georgia Tech, USA
Liang-Jie Zhang (Co-chair)   Shenzhen University, China

EDGE 2024 Program Committee

Xianghan Zheng   Fuzhou University, China
Le Chang   Guangdong University of Technology, China
Tao Han   New Jersey Institute of Technology, USA
Tessema Mengistu   Virginia Tech, USA
Rui André Oliveira   University of Lisbon, Portugal
Weichao Wang   University of North Carolina at Charlotte, USA
Mengjun Xie   University of Tennessee at Chattanooga, USA
Özgür Ertuğ   Gazi University, Turkey
Midori Sugaya   Shibaura Institute of Technology, Japan
Javid Taheri   Karlstad University, Sweden
Fangming Liu   Huazhong University of Science and Technology,
                                         China
Ahmed El Oualkadi   Abdelmalek Essaâdi University, Morocco

Conference Sponsor – Services Society

The Services Society (S2) is a non-profit professional organization that has been created to promote worldwide research and technical collaboration in services innovations among academia and industrial professionals. Its members are volunteers from industry and academia with common interests. S2 is registered in the USA as a "501(c) organization", which means that it is an American tax-exempt nonprofit organization. S2 collaborates with other professional organizations to sponsor or co-sponsor conferences and to promote an effective services curriculum in colleges and universities. The S2 initiates and promotes a "Services University" program worldwide to bridge the gap between industrial needs and university instruction.

The Services Sector accounted for 79.5% of the GDP of the USA in 2016. The world's most services-oriented economy, with services sectors accounting for more than 90% of GDP. The Services Society has formed 5 Special Interest Groups (SIGs) to support technology and domain-specific professional activities.

- Special Interest Group on Services Computing (SIG-SC)
- Special Interest Group on Big Data (SIG-BD)
- Special Interest Group on Cloud Computing (SIG-CLOUD)
- Special Interest Group on Artificial Intelligence (SIG-AI)
- Special Interest Group on Metaverse (SIG-Metaverse)

About the Services Conference Federation (SCF)

As the founding member of the Services Conference Federation (SCF), the first **International Conference on Web Services (ICWS)** was held in June 2003 in Las Vegas, USA. Meanwhile, the First International Conference on Web Services - Europe 2003 (ICWS-Europe 2003) was held in Germany in October 2003. ICWS-Europe 2003 was an extended event of the 2003 International Conference on Web Services (ICWS 2003) in Europe. In 2004, ICWS-Europe was changed to the European Conference on Web Services (ECOWS), which was held in Erfurt, Germany. Sponsored by the Services Society and Springer, SCF 2018 and SCF 2019 were held successfully in Seattle and San Diego, USA. SCF 2020 and SCF 2021 were held successfully online and in Shenzhen, China. SCF 2023 was held successfully in Hawaii, USA. To celebrate its 21st birthday, SCF 2024 was held on November 16–19, 2024, in Bangkok, Thailand.

In the past 21 years, the ICWS community has been expanded from Web engineering innovations to scientific research for the whole services industry. The service delivery platforms have been expanded to mobile platforms, Internet of Things, cloud computing, and edge computing. The services ecosystem has gradually been enabled, value added, and intelligence embedded through enabling technologies such as big data, artificial intelligence, and cognitive computing. In the coming years, all transactions with multiple parties involved will be transformed to blockchain.

Based on technology trends and best practices in the field, the Services Conference Federation (SCF) will continue serving as the conference umbrella's code name for all services-related conferences. SCF 2024 defined the future of New ABCDE (AI, Blockchain, Cloud, BigData & IOT) and entered the AIGC for Services Era. The theme of SCF 2024 was **AI-Generated Services**. We are very proud to announce that SCF 2024's 10 co-located theme topic conferences were all centered around "services", while each focused on exploring different themes (web-based services, cloud-based services, Big Data-based services, services innovation lifecycle, AI-driven ubiquitous services, blockchain-driven trust service ecosystems, industry-specific services and applications, and emerging service-oriented technologies).

- Bigger Platform: The 10 collocated conferences (SCF 2024) were sponsored by the Services Society which is the world-leading not-for-profit organization (501(c)(3)) dedicated to the service of more than 30,000 worldwide Services Computing researchers and practitioners. A bigger platform means bigger opportunities for all volunteers, authors, and participants. Meanwhile, Springer provided sponsorship of the best paper awards and other professional activities. All the 10 conference proceedings of SCF 2024 will be published by Springer and indexed in the ISI Conference Proceedings Citation Index (included in Web of Science), Engineering Index EI (Compendex and Inspec databases), DBLP, Google Scholar, IO-Port, MathSciNet, Scopus, and ZBlMath.
- Brighter Future: While celebrating the 2024 version of ICWS, SCF 2024 highlighted the International Conference on AI and Multimodal Services (AIMS 2024) to build

the fundamental infrastructure for enabling AIGC services ecosystems. It will also lead our community members to create their own brighter future.

- Better Model: SCF 2024 will continue to leverage the invented Conference Blockchain Model (CBM) to innovate the organizing practices for all the 10 theme conferences. Senior researchers in the field are welcome to submit proposals to serve as CBM Ambassador for an individual conference to start better interactions during your leadership role in organizing future SCF conferences.

Contents

A Measurement Inaccuracy Monitoring Method of Electricity Meter Based on Intelligent Measuring Switch

Mingfeng Shi[✉], Yonggen Gan, Yuke Zhao, Feifei Liu, and Weihuang Wen

China Gridcom Co., Ltd, Shenzhen 518109, China
shimingfeng@sgchip.sgcc.com.cn

Abstract. Aiming at the problem that the electricity meter in the metering cabinet can not be found in time when the measurement inaccuracy occurs in the long-term operation process, a method for monitoring the measurement inaccuracy of the electricity meter based on the intelligent measuring switch is proposed. The common causes of inaccurate measurement of electricity meter are analyzed. The method of judging the inaccurate measurement of electric energy based on intelligent measuring switch is designed, and the on-line monitoring process of inaccurate measurement is constructed. The effectiveness and feasibility of the proposed method are verified by real experiments. This method can predict the measurement abnormality of the electricity meter in advance and provide technical support for the management of the electric energy metering cabinet.

Keywords: Metering Cabinet · Intelligent Measuring Switch · Electricity Meter · Measurement Inaccuracy · On-line Monitoring

1 Introduction

With the deepening of the construction of the new power system, the intelligent level of the metering cabinet has been significantly improved. The overall metering management with the metering cabinet as the unit replaces the traditional large-area management, and monitors and responds all kinds of power parameters, line loss data, power theft and fault points in the cabinet in real time, so as to realize the full-range interconnection and perception of the low-voltage distribution station area, and enable the construction of a new power system [1, 2]. The metering cabinet of the electricity meter is mainly used to install the electricity meter and other equipment. It is the demarcation point of the property right between the power supply company and the user equipment. The inlet switch of the metering cabinet is gradually replaced by the ordinary molded case circuit breaker into the intelligent measuring switch. The intelligent measuring switch reads the data information of the voltage, current and power of the electricity meter in the metering cabinet, and provides data support for the inaccuracy analysis. The intelligent measuring switch has a high-precision current sensor and a measurement unit, which can realize the normal connection and breaking of the distribution and utilization lines, as well

© The Author(s), under exclusive license to Springer Nature Switzerland AG 2025
J. Zeng and L.-J. Zhang (Eds.): EDGE 2024, LNCS 15424, pp. 1–13, 2025.
https://doi.org/10.1007/978-3-031-77069-2_1

as overload and short-circuit protection functions, and can realize the local or remote interaction of measurement data. The remote interaction mainly communicates with the acquisition terminal through the HPLC and HRF (high-speed power line carrier communication and high-speed radio frequency communication), and then the acquisition terminal interacts the data with the master station through the 4G/5G wireless network [3, 4]. The local interaction mainly communicates with the electricity meter through Bluetooth or RS485. Figure 1 is the network communication architecture diagram.

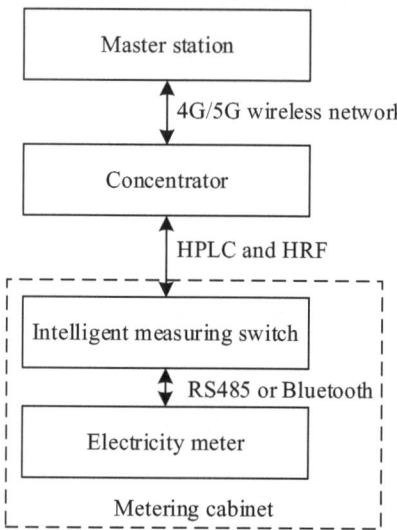

Fig. 1. The Network Communication Architecture Diagram

In the current metering cabinet, the replacement of the electricity meter is mainly based on the service life of the meter. For example, the service life of the electricity meter is 10 years, and the power management department carries out the replacement of the electricity meter according to the life cycle table. Reference [5] analyzed the causes of inaccurate measurement of electricity meter in practical application. Reference [6] collected daily power consumption through intelligent circuit breakers for big data edge computing to monitor inaccuracy metering devices. Reference [7] presents a methodology for assessing measurement inaccuracies utilizing a neural network model, specifically addressing the issue of abnormal voltage sampling resistance in electricity meters. Through the study of electrical topology technology, reference [8] designed an electrical topology identification scheme based on intelligent measuring switch. Based on the current research and technology, this paper mainly analyzes the causes of measurement inaccuracy and the analysis of inaccuracy through big data. There is no research on the analysis of the measurement inaccuracy of the electricity meter by using the intelligent measuring switch from the perspective of the whole cabinet of the metering cabinet and the realization of the information management of the mass metering cabinet in the low voltage station area.

Based on the intelligent measuring switch, this paper uses its total incoming line measurement to collect the voltage, current, power and electric quantity of the electricity meter in the metering cabinet for analysis and discrimination, and designs the intelligent measuring switch to monitor the on-line measurement error scheme of the electricity meter, which can provide strong support for the intelligent and refined construction of the metering cabinet, line loss analysis and stealing inspection [9].

2 Cause Analysis of Measurement Inaccuracy

According to the operation principle and application scenario of the electricity meter, the main reasons for the measurement inaccuracy of the electricity meter are the following four categories, namely, the instability of the measurement chip reference voltage, the abnormal sampling resistance, the error of the calibration table parameters and the poor contact. Figure 2 is the definition of the measurement chip pin.

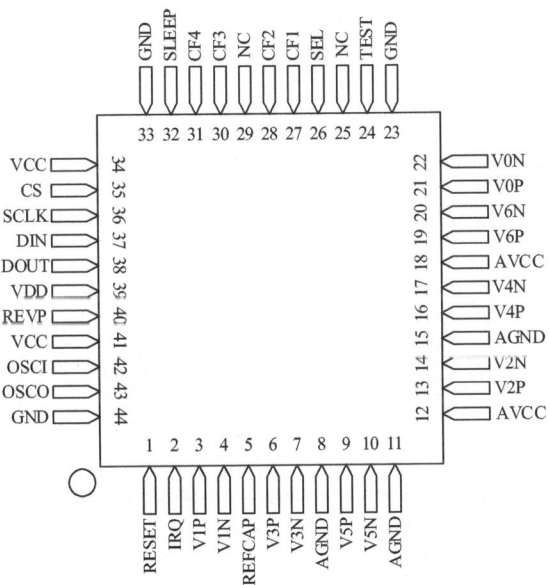

Fig. 2. Measurement Chip Pin Definition

2.1 The Measurement Chip Reference Voltage Instability of Electricity Meter

According to the definition of the measurement chip pin commonly used in the electricity meter, each measurement chip has a reference voltage pin, which is mainly used to provide the reference value of the measurement chip sampling, and is decoupled by using a capacitance of 10 μF capacitor in parallel with a 0.1 μF capacitor. The circuit diagram is shown in Fig. 3.

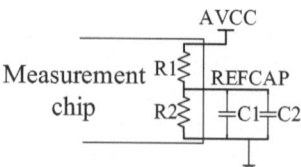

Fig. 3. Measurement Chip Reference Voltage Circuit Schematic

The reference voltage of the measurement chip is obtained by dividing the AVCC voltage supplied to the measurement chip by the equivalent R1 and R2 resistors inside the chip, and then decoupled by two external decoupling capacitors to ensure low ripple and stability of the reference voltage. Due to the differences in the production process of the electricity meter and the materials of the capacitors C1 and C2, some electricity meters C1 and C2 will have false welding and failure during long-term use. When the equivalent impedance of one of the capacitors is reduced, it can be seen from Fig. 3 that the voltage value of the REFCAP pin will be reduced. When the reference voltage is reduced, if the calibration table parameters do not change, the value after voltage sampling will increase. Once the accuracy level of the electricity meter is exceeded, the measurement will be inaccurate.

2.2 Abnormal Sampling Resistance of Electricity Meter

The voltage and current sampling circuit schematics of the electricity meter are shown in Figs. 4 and 5.

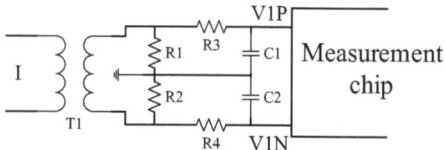

Fig. 4. Current Sampling Circuit Schematic

In Fig. 4, T1 is the current transformer, I represents the current flowing through the electricity meter, and Is is used to represent the secondary current of the current transformer. At this time, the sampling value of the current is equal to Is × (R1 + R2). When the accuracy of R1, R2 and T1 changes over time and exceeds the error, the measurement inaccuracy will occur.

In Fig. 5, the fire line L and zero line N of the AC voltage send the analog signal to the measurement chip for sampling by means of resistance divider. The sampling value of the measurement chip voltage is equal to [R9 / (R1 + R2 + … + R9)] × U, U is the voltage of the mains. According to the formula, changing any resistance value will affect the sampling of the voltage. When the change of resistance makes the measurement accuracy of the meter change, the measurement will be inaccurate.

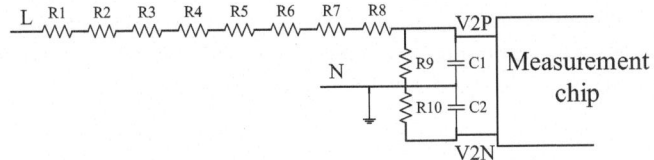

Fig. 5. Voltage Sampling Circuit Schematic

2.3 Electricity Meter Calibration Parameters

Before the electricity meter leaves the factory, it will be calibrated. Generally, two methods are used for calibration, including power calibration method and error calibration method. The specific process is shown in Fig. 6. Firstly, the electricity meter initializes the calibration register, that is, emptying the calibration register, starting the calibration, configuring the ADC gain, HFConst parameters, current parameters, etc., and calibrating the voltage, current and power factor through the standard power source. The calibration parameters are stored in the EEPROM and the calibration is completed.

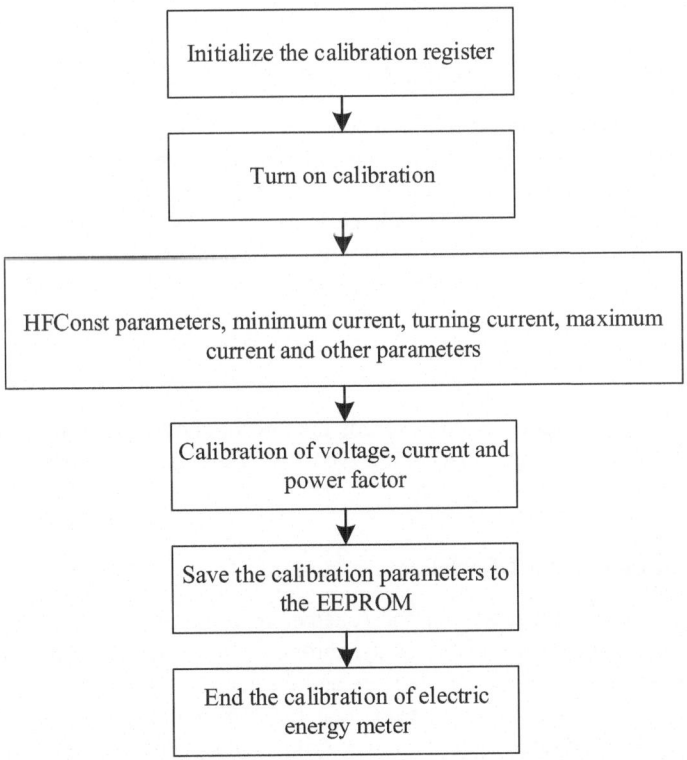

Fig. 6. Flowchart for the Application of Electricity Meter Calibration Parameters

From the calibration process, it can be seen that in the long-term operation of the electricity meter, if the calibration parameters are abnormal and exceed the accuracy level of the electricity meter, there will be a measurement error.

2.4 Poor Electrical Connection

Due to the aging of cables or copper bars in the metering cabinet, the loosening and shedding of the inlet and outlet terminals of the electricity meter, the problem of inaccurate metering of the electricity meter will also occur.

3 Discrimination Method of Metering Inaccuracy of Electricity Meter

According to the reasons for the measurement error of the electricity meter, in order to monitor the measurement accuracy of the electricity meter in real time, discover the abnormal problem of electricity consumption in time, reduce the waste of resources and reduce the loss of customers or electric companies, the measurement error can be judged by the following four methods [10–12].

3.1 Voltage Inaccuracy Discrimination Method

By configuring the acquisition task and scheme, according to the internal file of the intelligent measuring switch, the clock synchronization of the electricity meter in the metering cabinet is carried out periodically, and the real-time voltage value of the voltage $U_{QS}(t1)$ of the whole cabinet and the voltage value of the electricity meter in the cabinet $U_{Wh}^{i}(t1)$ are collected at time t1, i = 1 represents the first electricity meter in the metering cabinet, and the value of i varies with the number of electricity meters in the metering cabinet.

$$\Delta U = U_{QS}(t1) - U_{Wh}^{i}(t1) \tag{1}$$

In Eq. 1, when the value of ΔU exceeds the threshold of measurement inaccuracy, the electricity meter files and inaccuracy events are saved locally and reported to the master station.

3.2 Current Inaccuracy Discrimination Method

By configuring the acquisition task and scheme, according to the internal file of the intelligent measuring switch, the clock synchronization of the electricity meter in the metering cabinet is periodically carried out, and the zero crossing detection function of the high-speed power line carrier is used to realize the A, B and C three-phase phases of each single-phase electricity meter in the metering cabinet. The real-time current value of the total current $I_{QS}(t1)$ of each phase in the metering cabinet at time t1 and the current value of the electricity meter of each phase in the metering cabinet are collected.

$$\Delta I = I_{QS}(t1) - \sum_{i=1}^{n} I_{Wh}^{i}(t1) \tag{2}$$

In Eq. 2, when the value of ΔI exceeds the threshold of measurement inaccuracy, the electricity meter files and inaccuracy events are saved locally and reported to the master station. This method can only identify the inaccuracy of the electricity meter of a certain phase in the metering cabinet, and can not locate the specific electricity meter measurement inaccuracy.

3.3 Active Power Inaccuracy Discrimination Method

The discrimination method of active power inaccuracy is similar to that of power loss. Firstly, the clock synchronization is carried out, and then the phase identification of the electricity meter in the metering cabinet is carried out. The active power of each phase of the intelligent measuring switch is compared with the sum of the active power of the electricity meter in the metering cabinet on this phase.

$$\Delta P = P_{QS}(t1) - \sum_{i=1}^{n} P_{Wh}^i(t1) \tag{3}$$

In Eq. 3, when the value of ΔP exceeds the threshold of measurement inaccuracy, the electricity meter files and inaccuracy events are saved locally and reported to the master station.

3.4 Total Active Electrical Energy Inaccuracy Discrimination Method

The method for determining the inaccuracy of total active electrical energy is similar to the method for determining current inaccuracy. First, clock synchronization is performed, and then phase identification is performed on the electricity meters inside the metering cabinet. The active total energy data during a certain freezing period of the switch is measured and compared with the sum of the total active energy data of the electricity meters in that phase.

$$\Delta W = W_{QS}(T1) - \sum_{i=1}^{n} W_{Wh}^i(T1) \tag{4}$$

In Eq. 4, when the value of ΔW exceeds the threshold for measurement inaccuracy, the electricity meter records and inaccuracy events are saved locally and reported to the master station.

4 On-line Monitoring Process for Meter Inaccuracy

According to the cause of measurement inaccuracy and measurement inaccuracy discrimination method, this paper designs the on-line inaccuracy monitoring process based on the intelligent measuring switch, which is shown in Fig. 7. First of all, the intelligent measuring switch searches the electricity meters in the metering cabinet through RS485 communication, and stores the communication address of the searched electricity meters. Based on HPLC's voltage over-zero detection technology, it obtains the phase of the power meter in the file from the concentrator to determine the specific phase of the power meter in A, B, and C. The phase identification result is stored. By reading the data of voltage, current, active power and active total electric energy of itself and the electricity meter in the metering cabinet, according to the measurement inaccuracy discrimination method of the electricity meter proposed in this paper, it periodically judges whether the electricity meter exceeds the inaccuracy threshold, and if it exceeds the threshold, it goes through 2 more times of the same acquisition and judgment (for determining the inaccuracy event in order to prevent the false alarms), and if both results exceed the threshold, the inaccuracy event will be stored locally, alarmed by the intelligent measuring switch alarm indicator, and the inaccuracy data and event will be uploaded to the master station. If the thresholds are not exceeded, the intelligent measuring switch continues to monitor inaccuracy and collect data.

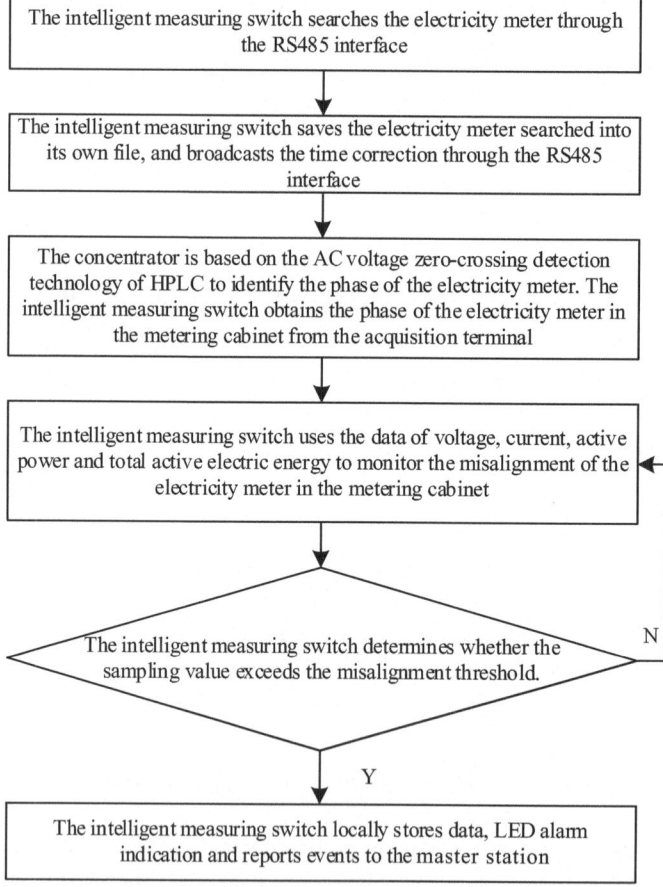

Fig. 7. Flowchart for On-line Monitoring of Electricity Meter

5 Experimental Validation and Analysis

There are mainly application scenarios such as charging pile, industrial power consumption and general residential power consumption in the metering cabinet under the power distribution area, and measurement inaccuracy monitoring experiments are conducted for these three types of application scenarios respectively.

5.1 Electric Vehicle Charging Pile Monitoring Experiment

The environment is built according to Fig. 8, and the experimental apparatus mainly includes: 1 computer with simulation master software installed, 1 I-type concentrator, one set of metering cabinet (including 1 intelligent measuring switch, 1 single-phase electricity meter, and 1 outlet switch), one set of 7kW AC charging pile, and 1 electric vehicle.

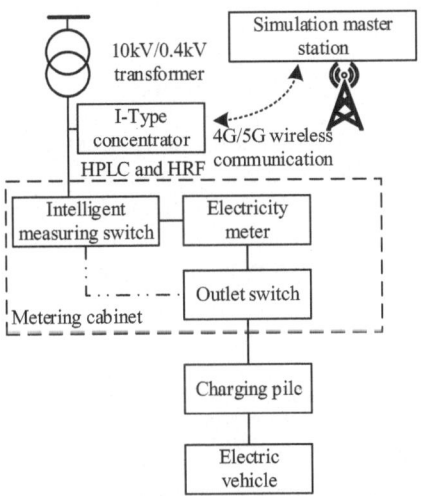

Fig. 8. Wiring diagram of the charging pile monitoring experiment

First of all, the concentrator, the intelligent measuring switch and the electricity meter are networked through HPLC and HRF, the intelligent measuring switch obtains the phases installed in the electricity meter in the metering cabinet from the concentrator, and the concentrator communicates with the simulated master station through 4G/5G wireless network to monitor the measurement inaccuracy event through the simulated master station. When the intelligent measuring switch can read its own voltage, current, power and electricity data normally, it simulates the electricity meter measurement inaccuracy event, and the specific test data are shown in Table 1. It changes the voltage sampling resistance of the electricity meter to simulate the voltage inaccuracy; it disconnects the cable between the electricity meter and the outlet switch, and connects the measurement switch and the outlet switch directly to simulate the inaccuracy of the current, the active power, and the total active electricity.

Table 1. Electric vehicle charging pile monitoring experiment

Serial No	Test items	Number of tests	Number of successful detected measurement inaccuracy	Success rate in detecting measurement inaccuracy
1	Voltage inaccuracy	500 times	500 times	100%
2	Current inaccuracy	500 times	497 times	99.4%
3	Active power inaccuracy	500 times	498 times	99.6%
4	Total active electrical energy inaccuracy	500 times	500 times	100%

5.2   Industrial Electricity Monitoring Experiment

According to Fig. 9 for the construction of the environment, the experimental apparatus mainly includes: 1 computer installed with simulation master software, 1 I-type concentrator, one set of metering cabinet (including 1 intelligent measuring switch, 3 single-phase electricity meters, 3 outlet switches), a few lighting fixtures, one set of 5.5kW industrial motors, one set of 9kW air conditioners.

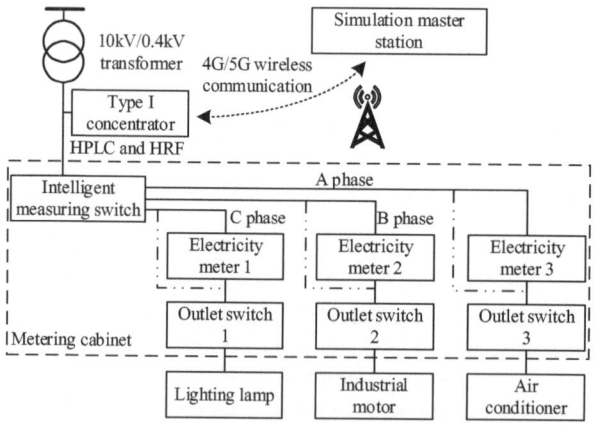

Fig. 9. Wiring diagram of industrial electricity monitoring experiment

Networking steps are the same as Sect. 5.1, the specific test data are shown in Table 2, voltage inaccuracy by modifying the resistance of the electricity meter 1, other inaccuracy by disconnecting the cable line between the electricity meter 1 and the outlet switch 1, and connecting directly to the intelligent measuring switch and the outlet switch 1 for testing, and the testing of the industrial motor and air conditioner is the same as the testing of the lighting lamp.

Table 2. Industrial electricity monitoring experiment.

Serial No	Test items	Number of tests	Number of successful detected measurement inaccuracy	Success rate in detecting measurement inaccuracy
1	Voltage inaccuracy	500 times	499 times	99.8%
2	Current inaccuracy	500 times	497 times	99.4%
3	Active power inaccuracy	500 times	499 times	99.8%
4	Total active electrical energy inaccuracy	500 times	500 times	100%

5.3 Residential Electricity Monitoring Experiment

The environment is built according to Fig. 10, and the experimental apparatus mainly includes: 1 computer installed with simulation master software, 1 I-Type concentrator, one set of metering cabinet (including 1 intelligent measuring switch, 3 single-phase electricity meters, and 3 outlet switches), one set of 3.5kW air conditioner, one set of Class 1 energy-efficiency refrigerator, and one set of Class 1 energy-efficiency washing machine.

The networking steps are the same as in Sect. 5.1, and the specific test data are shown in Table 3. Voltage inaccuracy is tested by modifying the resistance of the electricity meter 1, and other inaccuracy are tested by disconnecting the cable wires between the electricity meter 1 and the outlet switch 1, and directly connecting the intelligent measuring switch and the outlet switch 1.

From the analysis of the above experimental data, it can be seen that the method designed in this paper is able to accurately realize the measurement inaccuracy judgment of electricity meters in application scenarios such as electric vehicle charging piles, industrial electricity consumption and residential electricity consumption by means of the intelligent measuring switch, and the inaccuracy detection success rate reaches more than 99.2%.

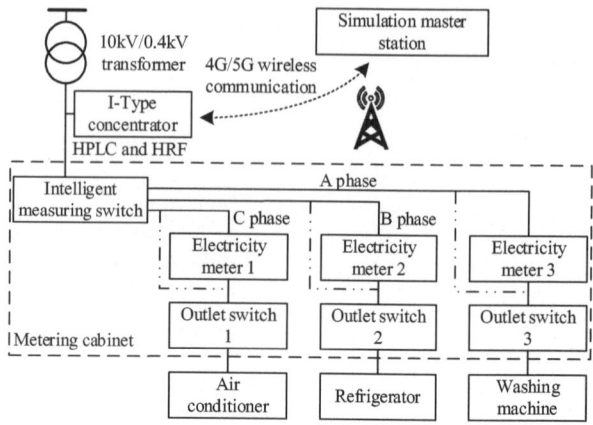

Fig. 10. Wiring diagram of residential electricity monitoring experiment

Table 3. Residential electricity monitoring experiment.

Serial No	Test items	Number of tests	Number of successful detected measurement inaccuracy	Success rate in detecting measurement inaccuracy
1	Voltage inaccuracy	500 times	497 times	99.4%
2	Current inaccuracy	500 times	496 times	99.2%
3	Active power inaccuracy	500 times	498 times	99.6%
4	Total active electrical energy inaccuracy	500 times	500 times	100%

6 Conclusions

Based on the intelligent measuring switch, this paper designs a method for monitoring the measurement inaccuracy of electricity meters. Firstly, according to the engineering application experience, the reasons for the inaccuracy of electricity meter are analyzed from the hardware, software and on-site installation scenarios. Through the reasons, the specific performance after the inaccuracy of electricity meter is found out, and the on-line monitoring process of the inaccuracy of electricity meters is designed. Then, the real experiment is carried out on three application scenarios of electric vehicle charging pile, industrial electricity and residential electricity. The success rate of measurement inaccuracy monitoring of the proposed method is verified by experiments. According to the experimental results, the proposed method has strong feasibility and practicability. It can improve the discrimination accuracy of electricity meter measurement error.

References

1. Wei, W., Li, F., Li, L., et al.: Digital watt-hour meter running performance analysis and evaluation at non-standard load conditions. Sci. Technol. Eng. **18**(9), 94–100 (2018)
2. Lai, G.: Data – driven online monitoring method of running state of electricity meter. Electr. Measur. Instrum. **60**(4), 193–200 (2023)
3. Wang, S., Rao, Y., Chen, H., et al.: A monitoring method of voltage misalignment for the residential electricity meter based on HPLC platform. Sci. Technol. Eng. **59**(10), 154–160 (2022)
4. Zhang, K., Zhang, J., Du, W., et al.: Research on accurately identifying electricity stealing users based on linear regression. Electron. Des. Eng. **31**(17), 51–55 (2023)
5. Zhang, Z.: Analysis method of inaccurate measurement of smart meter. Electr. Eng. **22**(5), 85–88 (2021)
6. Li, Q., Wu, Y., Shi, J., et al.: Big data-based monitoring technology for smart circuit breaker line loss and measurement misalignment instruments. New Technol. New Prod. Chin. **17**, 1–4 (2023)
7. Zhu, Z., Chen, H., Jiang, C., et al.: Study of measurement inaccuracy for an electric energy meter with abnormal voltage sampling resistance. J. South-Central Minzu Univ. (Nat. Sci. Ed.) **41**(6), 682–688 (2022)
8. Xiong, D., Xu, W., Xiong, S., et al.: Research on topology recognition technology of intelligent measuring switch. Mod. Electron. Tech. **46**(8), 130–136 (2023)
9. Liang, X., Liu, S., Li, T., et al.: Design of an object-oriented security communication protocol for electricity information system. Electr. Meas. Instrum. **56**(4), 80–87 (2019)
10. Chen, W., Tian, L., Gao, F., et al.: Remote metering monitoring and evaluation of urban electric vehicle charging pile research on application of analysis system. Chin. Measur. Test **49**(z1), 151–157 (2023)
11. Jin, W., Li, F., Zhou, L.: Ultra short-term industrial power prediction based on density peak clustering. Comput. Simul. **40**(2), 84–88 (2023)
12. Li, B., Li, F., Zhou, D., et al.: Research on event monitoring and load feature extraction method based on residential electricity consumption data. J. Taiyuan Univ. Technol. **55**(1), 2–11 (2024)

Demographic Change, Housing Prices and Household Debt Sustainability: Empirical Analysis Using Dynamic System GMM Model and Mediation Effect Model

Lei Yu[1], Wenxian Zhou[2(✉)], Yujie Lin[3], Xinlong Yang[4], and Jue Wang[5]

[1] Xi'an University of Technology, Xi'an, China
[2] Xi'an International University, Xi'an, China
chsdcy@xaut.edu.cn
[3] Hunan University, Changsha, China
[4] Shenzhen Institute of Information Technology, Shenzhen, China
[5] Jiangsu University, Zhenjiang, China

Abstract. This paper explores the impact of demographic changes on the sustainability of household liabilities, which is crucial for adjusting the effects of demographic shifts and stabilizing household debt levels. Using inter-provincial panel data and econometric models, including fixed effects, systematic GMM, and mediation effect models, the study examines how demographic structure affects household debt sustainability. It finds that the natural population structure has a more significant impact than social or spatial factors. Key results include: (1) higher child and old-age dependency ratios worsen debt sustainability, with regional variations; (2) a favorable gender ratio improves debt sustainability, particularly in the eastern regions; (3) higher income ratios for home-purchase and consumption expenditures, along with GDP growth, benefit debt sustainability, while financial security income has a negative effect; (4) rising house prices mediate the relationship between demographic changes and debt sustainability. The study recommends policy improvements such as incentives for multiple births and enhanced social security.

Keywords: Household Debt Sustainability · Demographics · House Prices · Mediating Effects

1 Introduction

In recent years, the scale of household indebtedness in China has continued to expand, with the high level of debt in the household sector becoming a hidden risk to China's economic operation and financial system. According to data from the People's Bank of China (PBoC), the balance of individual housing loans in China grew by 27.44% from 2019 to 2021, far exceeding the growth rate of household disposable income. Data from the National Center for Balance Sheet Studies (CNBS) also shows that China's household leverage ratio has been hovering around 62% since the first quarter of 2022,

J. Zeng and L.-J. Zhang (Eds.): EDGE 2024, LNCS 15424, pp. 14–32, 2025.
https://doi.org/10.1007/978-3-031-77069-2_2

with household debt remaining high. The excessive accumulation of debt has once again triggered widespread concern in the community about the sustainability of household debt.

Demographic structure is one of the important factors affecting household debt. Since the founding of the People's Republic of China, the trend of population growth has changed considerably as people's standard of living has risen, medical conditions have improved, and fertility policies have been adjusted. The pattern of population reproduction has evolved from the primitive type of "high-high-low" to the traditional type of "high-low-high," and then to the modern type of "low-low-low." The changing demographic structure not only affects the sustainable development of the national economy but also alters the structure of household consumption and output levels.

Currently, China has entered a new normal period characterized by the coexistence of "aging" and "childlessness." This dual population dependency reduces family savings (Liu et al., 2021) and increases the economic burden on families. By studying the relationship between demographic structure and household debt, it is possible to understand more systematically and comprehensively which indicators of demographic structure impact household liabilities. This understanding can help identify the pathways through which demographic structure affects household debt, providing a reference for adjusting demographic policies and improving the sustainability of household liabilities.

Most existing literature explores the impact of demographic structure on household debt, but few address the sustainability of household indebtedness across natural, social, and spatial dimensions. This paper makes three key contributions: (1) It incorporates sex ratio and population mobility into the analysis of demographic structure, providing a more comprehensive examination of the impact of demographic changes on debt sustainability. (2) It investigates the regional variability of demographic impacts on household debt across eastern, central, and western China. (3) It examines the combined effects of pediatric and elderly populations on household debt, with a focus on total population dependency ratios. Additionally, this paper considers the mediating role of housing prices, establishing a dynamic mediation model to explore both direct and indirect effects of demographic changes on debt sustainability. These insights offer valuable policy recommendations for improving the sustainability of household liabilities.

2 Literature Review and Theoretical Analysis

2.1 Population Age Structure and Household Debt Sustainability

Existing research on population structure and household debt has focused on the natural, social and spatial aspects of the population. First, concerning the natural structure, the age structure of the population has provided significant insights into its impact on household debt. Older individuals are less likely to incur debt than younger people (Fabbri & Padula, 2004). When aging exceeds a certain threshold, it accelerates the rapid growth of household indebtedness (Liu et al., 2020). Additionally, population aging contributes to a decline in house prices, increasing the risk of household indebtedness (Tong & Zhang, 2018).

In terms of Impact of Child-rearing and Old-age Dependency Ratios on Household Debt, this is mainly divided into three areas:(1)A decline in the child-rearing ratio and an increase in the old-age dependency ratio leads to higher household leverage (Guo et al., 2015). This effect primarily influences on household borrowing demand through income distribution (Zhou & Wang, 2017). (2) An increase in the child-rearing ratio and a decline in the old-age dependency ratio raise both the probability of households holding liabilities and the size of liabilities (Yang & Zhu, 2016). (3) Both ratios increase the probability of indebtedness in the household, exhibiting regional heterogeneity (Hu et al, 2015). In studies examining the gender structure of the population, females tend to adopt a more cautious and conservative approach to debt financing, potentially reducing household debt risk (Jianakoplos & Bernasek, 1998).

As the foundation of the social structure, the family plays multiple roles, including supporting the elderly and raising and educating children. In China, where the social economy and welfare system are still developing, the increase in the elderly population has raised the consumption related to support, medical care, and health care. Given a fixed income, families often resort to borrowing to cover these additional expenditures. Moreover, China's "one-child policy" has led families to shift their investment in children from quantity to quality (Wang et al., 2020). When income is insufficient to cover the costs of children's education and support, families may incur debt to smooth consumption (Guo et al., 2015). Consequently, increases in both the child-rearing and the elderly-rearing ratios elevate the debt burden of the households, potentially exacerbating the sustainability of the household indebtedness. The total dependency ratio, combined measure of the child-rearing and old-age dependency ratios (Liu et al., 2021), reflects the extent of the dependency burden the working population must bear. Household with low incomes or limited savings might seek relief through borrowing, thus a rise in the total dependency ratio can increase household indebtedness and challenge the sustainability of this indebtedness. Based on this analysis, research hypothesis H1a is formulated.

H1a: Rising child, old-age and total dependency ratios will exacerbate the sustainability of the household's indebtedness.

The gender ratio is an important factor influencing household asset-liability decisions (Chen, & Li, 2011). Women tend to be more risk-averse compared to men, displaying a more cautious and conservative attitude toward liabilities. Furthermore, the worsening gender imbalance in China, characterized by more men and fewer women, places men at a disadvantage in the marriage market. Consequently, families with sons are more inclined to invest in housing, which serves both as a residence and as an investment, in anticipation of improving their sons' prospects in future marriages (Li & Wu, 2017). This dynamic increases households' exposure to debt risk and deepen the sustainability challenges of household indebtedness. Based on this understanding, research hypothesis H1b is formulated:

H1b: Gender ratios exacerbate the challenges to the sustainability of household debt.

2.2 Family Size and Sustainability of Household Indebtedness

Research on demographic social structure indicates that population size is positively associated with household debt demand, with notable regional differences (Crook, 2001; Liu & Zhou, 2012). Worthington (2006) pointed out that the number of children is positively correlated with financial stress related to household debt in Australian households. In examining education structure, it has been found that households with higher levels of education tend to borrow more rationally due to their cautious approach to risk (Campbell & Cocco, 2003). This rational borrowing behavior is attributed to the higher likelihood of educated groups identifying favorable investment opportunities and securing loans compared to their less educated counterparts (Song et al., 2017). However, some scholars contend that there may be an inverse relationship between education level and household indebtedness (Zhu & Xia, 2018).

The seventh population census in China in 2020 revealed an average family size 2.62 persons, indicating aging population with fewer children and a trend towards smaller family size. Conversely, as family sizes become smaller and more nuclear, the number of members available to share risks decreases significantly, thereby weakening the household's ability to support elderly members without a corresponding increase in income. This trend towards "miniaturization" and "nuclearization" of households underscores the need to understand its implications on financial stability. Based on this analysis, the following research hypothesis is proposed:

H2: An increase in family size enhances the sustainability of household indebtedness.

2.3 Population Mobility and Household Debt Sustainability

Research on the impact of population spatial structure on household debt is limited. Wu & Zhang (2016) posit that increased population inflow to cities elevates housing prices, which can subsequently increase household debt. Saiz(2007) verifies that population mobility drives up housing prices through heightened demand, with rising house prices being a significant factor contributing to rising household leverage (Ruan et al., 2020). Population migration enhances household income levels, thereby improving households' risk resilience and deepening the sustainability of household liabilities. However, household expenditure on education, healthcare, and housing security varies with household registration differences. When a disparity between income and expenditure exists, household borrowing demand and debt size will escalate, further influencing the sustainability of household liabilities. Based on above analysis, the following research hypothesis H3 is proposed.

H3: Population mobility is positively related to the sustainability of household debt.

2.4 Intermediation Effects of House Prices

The relationship between house prices and household debt is primarily manifested through direct effect, collateral effects, and wealth effects. Firstly, the direct effect of high house prices on household debt occurs when households, lacking sufficient funds, resort to mortgage loans to purchase houses, thereby increasing household debt (Campbell & Cocco, 2007). Secondly, high house prices impact household debt through the collateralization effect, as increased housing collateral value encourages financial institutions to provide more housing loans (Igan & Ioungani, 2012). Lastly, house prices influence household debt through the wealth effect, rising house prices boost consumers' demand for investment in home purchases, increasing households' willingness to borrow and their risk appetite, leading to a rapid increase in household leverage (Zhou & Wang, 2019).

In China, the increasing degree of aging and the implementation of the "two-child policy" have heightened the financial burden on local governments. To address financial resource shortages, local governments have increased their disposable income through "land finance." However, the monopolization of land by local governments has significantly driven up housing prices (Xu et al., 2020), indirectly increasing the size of home mortgages. Additionally, as demographic structures shift, the varying proportions of different age groups generate diverse housing demands, stimulating housing prices. Fluctuations in house prices subsequently affect household debt through the mortgage and wealth effects. Based on this, the following research hypothesis H4 is proposed:

H4: House prices have a mediating effect on the influence of population age structure on the sustainability of household debt.

3 Data Selection and Modeling

3.1 Data Selection and Description of Variables

The data in this paper are sourced from various Chinese statistical yearbooks, the People's Bank of China, CEIC database, and Wind database, covering panel data from 31 provinces from 2013 to 2020, resulting in 248 observations over 8 years.

Explained Variables: The main variable is the sustainability of household debt, measured by the debt gap (Dg), which is the ratio of personal consumption loans to the total disposable income of the population.

Explanatory Variables: The core explanatory variables are categorized into:

- Child Dependency Ratio (Cdr): Ratio of population aged 0–14 to the working-age population.
- Old-age Dependency Ratio (Odr): Ratio of population aged 65 and above to the working-age population.
- Total Dependency Ratio (Tdr): Sum of Cdr and Odr.
- Sex Ratio (Sr): Number of males per 100 females.
- Family Size (Fs): Average number of people per household.
- Population Mobility Speed (Pms): Calculated as the change in permanent residents minus natural population growth, divided by the current year's permanent residents.

Mediating Variable: House Price (Hp) is calculated as the average sales price of commercial properties.

Control Variables:

- Ratio of Purchase Housing (Rph): Total housing sales to total disposable income.
- Consumption Expenditure Income Ratio (Ceir): Total consumption expenditure to total disposable income.
- Per Capita GDP Growth Rate (Pgdp): Growth rate calculated as (current year's GDP per capita - previous year's GDP per capita) / previous year's GDP per capita.
- Inflation Rate (Ir): Calculated from the CPI.

- Financial Security Income Ratio (Fsir): Ratio of local government expenditures on education, healthcare, and social security to total disposable income.

The meanings of the variables and data sources are shown in Table 1.

Table 1. Definition of Variables

Variables	Variable Descriptions
Debt Gap	Household sector debt/total disposable income of residents
Child Dependency Ratio	Population aged 0–14/labor force population
Old-age Dependency Ratio	Population aged 65 and above/labor force population
Total Dependency Ratio	Sum of child dependency ratio and old-age dependency ratio
Sex Ratio	Number of males per 100 females
Family Size	Average family size = total population/total number of households
Population Migration Speed	Population mobility speed = (permanent residents at the end of the current year − permanent residents at the end of the previous year − natural population growth for the current year) / permanent residents at the end of the current year
Ratio of Purchase Housing	Total housing sales/total disposable income of residents
Consumption Expenditure to Income Ratio	Total household consumption expenditure/total disposable income of residents
Per Capita GDP Growth Rate	(Per capita GDP for the current year - per capita GDP for the previous year)/per capita GDP for the previous year
Inflation Rate	Calculated through the Consumer Price Index (CPI)
Fiscal Security Income Ratio	Sum of local fiscal expenditures on education, healthcare, and social security employment/total disposable income of residents
House Price	Logarithm of the average sales price of commercial properties

3.2 Modeling

Baseline Regression Model

According to the research hypothesis, the model that reflects the relationship between demographic structure and the sustainability of household liabilities is constructed in Eq. (1). Meanwhile, considering that the sum of the child dependency ratio and the old-age dependency ratio is the total dependency ratio to avoid multicollinearity, this paper explores the impact of the total dependency ratio on the sustainability of household liabilities and constructs a model as shown in Eq. (2):

$$Dg_{it} = \alpha_1 Cdr_{it} + \alpha_2 Odr_{it} + \alpha_3 Sr_{it} + \alpha_4 Fs_{it} + \alpha_5 Pms_{it} + \alpha_6 X_{it} + c_i + \varepsilon_{it} \quad (1)$$

$$Dg_{it} = \beta_1 Tdr_{it} + \beta_2 Sr_{it} + \beta_3 Fs_{it} + \beta_4 Pms_{it} + \beta_5 X_{it} + c_i + \varepsilon_{it} \quad (2)$$

where the explanatory variables (Dg_{it}) denotes the household debt gap in the region i in year t; the explanatory variables are demographic, including the child dependency ratio (Cdr_{it}), the old-age dependency ratio (Odr_{it}), the total dependency ratio (Tdr_{it}), the sex ratio (Sr_{it}), the family size (Fs_{it}), and the rate of population migration in the region i in year t (Pms_{it}); X_{it} is a set of control variables, i.e., The Ratio of Purchase Housing (Rph_{it}), Consumption Expenditure Income Ratio ($Ceir_{it}$), the growth rate of per capita GDP ($Pgdp_{it}$), the rate of inflation in year one (Ir_{it}), the ratio of income from financial security in the region i in year t ($Fsir_{it}$); c_i denotes an individual-effects intercept term; and ε_{it} is a random-error term.

Given that the impact of demographic change on the household debt gap may be a long-term dynamic process, this paper introduces a lagged period (Dg_{it-1}) of the household debt gap in Eqs. (1) and (2) and constructs a dynamic panel model for estimation, as shown in Eqs. (3) and (4):

$$Dg_{it} = \gamma_1 Dg_{it-1} + \gamma_2 Cdr_{it} + \gamma_3 Odr_{it} + \gamma_4 Sr_{it} + \gamma_5 Fs_{it} + \gamma_6 Pms_{it} + \gamma_7 X_{it} + c_i + \varepsilon_{it} \quad (3)$$

$$Dg_{it} = \delta_1 Dg_{it-1} + \delta_2 Tdr_{it} + \delta_3 Sr_{it} + \delta_4 Fs_{it} + \delta_5 Pms_{it} + \delta_6 X_{it} + c_i + \varepsilon_{it} \quad (4)$$

Considering the endogeneity problem of the lagged one period (Dg_{it-1}) introduced in the model with the random error term (ε_{it}), which can lead to biased estimation of the parameters, this paper adopts system GMM for the analysis to improve the efficiency of the estimation results.

Intermediation Effect Model

In order to test whether the mechanism of demographic structure on the household debt gap exists, this paper draws on the test method of the mediation model. It introduces the mediating variable of house price (Hp), and constructs the recursive Eqs. (5) to (7) to test the mechanism of demographic structure on the debt gap in the household.

$$Dg_{it} = \alpha_1 Cdr_{it}/Odr_{it} + \alpha_2 Sr_{it} + \alpha_3 Fs_{it} + \alpha_4 Pms_{it} + \alpha_5 X_{it} + c_i + \varepsilon_{it} \quad (5)$$

$$Hp_{it} = \beta_1 Cdr_{it}/Odr_{it} + \beta_2 Sr_{it} + \beta_3 Fs_{it} + \beta_4 Pms_{it} + \beta_5 X_{it} + c_i + \varepsilon_{it} \quad (6)$$

$$Dg_{it} = \gamma_1 Cdr_{it}/Odr_{it} + \gamma_2 Hp_{it} + \gamma_3 Sr_{it} + \gamma_4 Fs_{it} + \gamma_5 Pms_{it} + \gamma_6 X_{it} + c_i + \varepsilon_{it} \quad (7)$$

Given the lagged effects of the household debt gap, this paper constructs dynamic panel mediation effects as shown in Eqs. (8) to (10):

$$Dg_{it} = \delta_1 Dg_{it-1} + \delta_2 Cdr_{it}/Odr_{it} + \delta_3 Sr_{it} + \delta_4 Fs_{it} + \delta_5 Pms_{it} + \delta_6 X_{it} + c_i + \varepsilon_{it} \quad (8)$$

$$Hp_{it} = \omega_1 Hp_{it-1} + \omega_2 Cdr_{it}/Odr_{it} + \omega_3 Sr_{it} + \omega_4 Fs_{it} + \omega_5 Pms_{it} + \omega_6 X_{it} + c_i + \varepsilon_{it} \quad (9)$$

$$Dg_{it} = \varphi_1 Dg_{it-1} + \varphi_2 Cdr_{it}/Odr_{it} + \varphi_3 Hp_{it} + \varphi_4 Sr_{it} + \varphi_5 Fs_{it} + \varphi_6 Pms_{it} + \varphi_7 X_{it} + c_i + \varepsilon_{it} \quad (10)$$

where Dg_{it-1} represents the one-period lagged term of the household debt gap; Hp_{it} and Hp_{it-1} reflect current and lagged house prices, respectively.

4 Empirical Studies

4.1 Descriptive Analysis

As observed in Table 2, the debt gap in the household has further increased. Since 2013, household debt as a share of disposable income has been rising annually, reaching 151.29% in 2020. Additionally, the average level of the household debt gap has surpassed 50% across the study area. The mean value of the child dependency ratio is 0.2337, and the mean value of the old-age dependency ratio is 0.1497. This indicates that for every 100 working individuals, there are 23 adolescents aged 0 to 14 years and 15 elderly individuals aged 65 years and above dependent on them. The standard deviation of the child dependency ratio is approximately twice that of the old-age dependency ratio, suggesting that changes in the total dependency ratio are largely influenced by fluctuations in the child dependency ratio. The average sex ratio is 1.05, indicating a higher male population compared to the female population. Most families in the country are predominantly three-member households, with a maximum family size of four to five members. The rate of population migration in the country is highly variable, with a mean of -0.03%.

From the scatterplot of the key variables with the household debt gap, it can be observed that the old-age dependency ratio is positively related to the household debt gap. Similarly, the total dependency ratio and the sex ratio are positively related to the household debt gap. However, the relationship between the child dependency ratio and the household debt gap is not prominent in the scatterplot and requires further empirical analysis to be confirmed (Figs. 1, 2 3 and 4).

Table 2. Descriptive Statistics of Variables

Variables	Obs	Mean	Std. Dev	Min	Max
Dg	248	0.6343	0.2960	0.0253	1.5129
Cdr	248	0.2337	0.0646	0.1170	0.3840
Odr	248	0.1497	0.0381	0.0700	0.2550
Tdr	248	0.3833	0.0685	0.2270	0.5780
Sr	248	1.0495	0.0402	0.9637	1.2317
Fs	248	3.0055	0.3771	2.2200	4.1300
Pms	248	−0.0003	0.0083	−0.0323	0.0204
Rph	248	0.2810	0.2054	0.0287	2.8323
Ceir	248	0.7173	0.0536	0.5603	0.8941
Pgdp	248	0.0758	0.0361	−0.0394	0.2140
Ir	248	0.0211	0.0063	0.0060	0.0390
Fsir	248	0.2355	0.1277	0.0986	0.9663
Lnhp	248	8.8484	0.5094	8.1901	10.6616

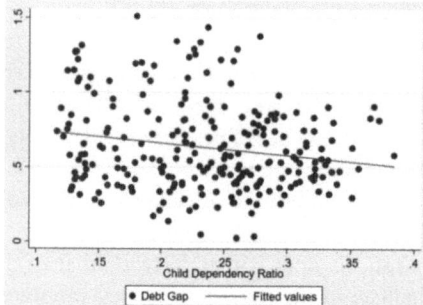

Fig. 1. Child Dependency Ratio and Debt Gap

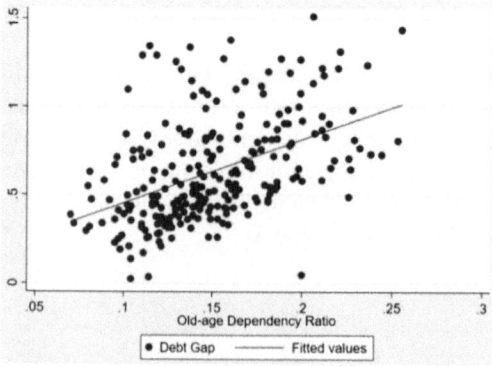

Fig. 2 Old-age Dependency Ratio and Debt Gap

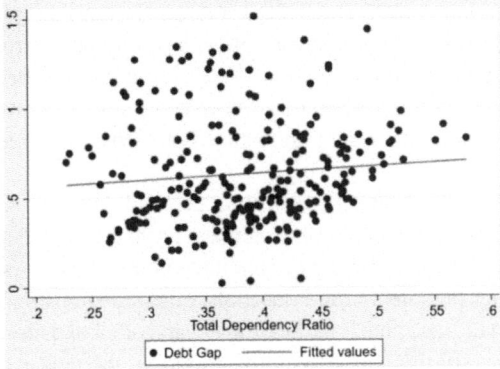

Fig. 3. Total Dependency Ratio and Debt Gap Fig. 4 Sex Rate and Debt Gap

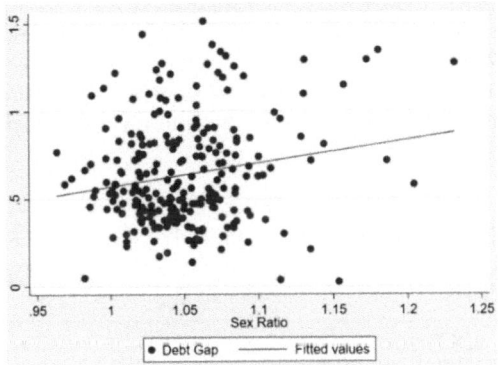

Fig. 4. Sex Rate and Debt Gap

4.2 Demographic Effects on the Sustainability of Household Indebtedness

Regression Results for the Full Sample

According to the results of the Hausman test, the chi-square statistic is 45.59, and the p-value is 0.0000, which strongly rejects the null hypothesis. Therefore, the fixed effects model is considered superior to the random effects model. Table 3 presents the regression estimation results using the fixed effects model, difference GMM, and system GMM models. As shown in the table, the effect of the child dependency ratio on the household debt gap is positive. It is not significant in the static panel model, but it becomes significant at the 1% level when regressed through the dynamic panel model. For every percentage point increase in the child support ratio, the debt gap of the household increases by 1.77 percentage points. This may be explained by the fact that, on the one hand, the "one-child policy" has led most households to shift their long-term investment in their children from quantity to quality, providing their children with more high-level and high-quality consumption, which promotes the growth of household consumption debt. On the other hand, since the implementation of the two-child policy in 2016, China's birth population has seen a significant increase. However, as China's infant and childcare service policies and regulations are not yet well-established, women in families often withdraw from the labor market due to childcare responsibilities, leading to an increase in expenditures along with a decrease in household income. When there is a gap between expenditures and household income, households tend to borrow to smooth consumption, resulting in an increase in total household debt and exacerbating the sustainability of household indebtedness.

The old-age dependency ratio raises the household debt gap and is significant at the 1% level. For every percentage point increase in the old-age dependency ratio, the debt gap of the household rises by 6.39 percentage points. This is because the increase in the number of older persons in the household raises the consumption burden on the household in terms of old-age pensions, healthcare, and other expenses. When the income is not sufficient to satisfy the increase in consumption, the debt gap of the household widens, deepening the sustainability issues of household indebtedness.

The effect of the total dependency ratio on the household debt gap is positive and significant at the 1% level. From columns (1) to (3) of Table 3, it can be seen that when both the child dependency ratio and the old-age dependency ratio increase by 1 percentage point, the old-age dependency ratio causes a larger increase in the household debt gap compared to the child dependency ratio. This is the main factor contributing to the positive effect of the total dependency ratio on the household debt gap, thus confirming Hypothesis H1a.

Table 3. Empirical Results of Static and Dynamic Panel Models

Variables	(1)	(2)	(3)	(4)	(5)	(6)
	Static Panel	Difference GMM	System GMM	Static Panel	Difference GMM	System GMM
$L.Dg$		0.2282***	0.2723***		0.2221***	0.3275***
		(0.0545)	(0.0148)		(0.0568)	(0.0300)
Tdr				3.5946***	4.9146***	4.7065***
				(0.3314)	(0.3378)	(0.3594)
Cdr	0.6711	3.3116***	1.7658***			
	(0.7667)	(0.6038)	(0.3157)			
Odr	5.5502***	5.7935***	6.3889***			
	(0.7030)	(0.5324)	(0.2553)			
Sr	0.555	0.5060*	1.9303***	0.5453	0.7392**	2.2833***
	(0.6261)	(0.2869)	(0.2156)	(0.6653)	(0.3554)	(0.3783)
Fs	−0.0432	0.0998*	0.0624	−0.0647	0.1346*	0.0780
	(0.0923)	(0.0595)	(0.0393)	(0.0995)	(0.0705)	(0.0630)
Pms	−4.2160*	0.6772	−1.0553	−5.3611***	1.0858	−0.7904
	(2.1826)	(2.2935)	(1.2860)	(1.7889)	(3.4116)	(1.3476)

(*continued*)

Table 3. (*continued*)

Variables	(1)	(2)	(3)	(4)	(5)	(6)
Control variables	controlled	controlled	controlled	controlled	controlled	controlled
_Cons	−0.4806	−2.5187***	−3.5113***	−0.7924	−2.7725***	−4.3094***
	(0.7173)	(0.4027)	(0.3911)	(0.7937)	(0.6054)	(0.6397)
Obs	248	186	186	248	186	186
Sargan		0.2129	0.4219		0.4057	0.2909
AR(1)		0.0670	0.0821		0.0579	0.0607
AR(2)		0.2756	0.3752		0.8006	0.5779

Note: Values in parentheses are t-values. ***, **, and * denote significance at the 1%, 5%, and 10% confidence levels, respectively

The effect of the sex ratio and family size on the household debt gap is positive, with the sex ratio being significant at the 1% level, while family size is not significant. The effect of the rate of population migration on the household debt gap is not significant, indicating that population migration is not a primary cause of the household debt gap. Although population migration may push up house prices, house price increases are not an absolute determinant of the increase in the household debt gap, so the speed of population migration does not necessarily trigger a change in the household debt gap, thus testing Hypothesis H1b.

Furthermore, the model passes a series of tests such as the Arellano-Bond serial autocorrelation test. In the serial autocorrelation test, the p-value of AR(1) is less than 0.1, and the p-value of AR(2) is greater than 0.1, indicating that there is first-order serial autocorrelation in the differential perturbation term and no second-order serial autocorrelation, which validates our moment equations. Additionally, the p-value of the Sargan over-identification test is not significant, indicating that there is no over-identification problem with the instrumental variables.

Heterogeneity Analysis at the Regional Level

Due to the significant differences in the demographics of China's eastern, central, and western regions, this paper aims to further explore whether regional-level differences exist in the impact of demographic changes on the household debt gap. To achieve this, the sample is divided into eastern, central, and western regions.[1] Given the potential endogeneity problem in the model, Baltagi (2006) argues that the Hausman test can only be used to select either a fixed-effects model or a random-effects model for estimation if endogeneity is addressed.

---

[1] The eastern region comprises 11 provinces and municipalities: Beijing, Tianjin, Hebei, Liaoning, Shanghai, Jiangsu, Zhejiang, Fujian, Shandong, Guangdong, and Hainan. The central and western regions encompass 20 provinces and municipalities: Shanxi, Jilin, Heilongjiang, Anhui, Jiangxi, Henan, Hubei, Hunan, Inner Mongolia, Sichuan, Chongqing, Guizhou, Yunnan, Tibet, Shaanxi, Gansu, Qinghai, Ningxia, Xinjiang, and Guangxi.

Therefore, in this paper, the endogeneity problem within the model is first addressed. The results of the Hausman test show that the chi-square statistic is 9.81 and the p-value is 0.4572, which supports the null hypothesis, indicating that the EC2SLS model should be selected for estimation. To ensure the robustness of the results, an additional endogeneity test was conducted on the model. The results of the Hausman test showed that the chi-square statistic was 113.15 with a p-value of 0.0000, strongly rejecting the null hypothesis and suggesting that there is indeed an endogeneity problem in the model.

Table 4 reports the regional differences in the impact of demographic structure on the household debt gap.

Table 4. Regional Differences in The Impact of Demographics on The Sustainability of Household Indebtedness

Variables	Eastern Area	Eastern Area	Central & Western Area	Central & Western Area
	RE	EC2SLS	RE	EC2SLS
Cdr	1.5704*	1.6410	0.5000	0.8488*
	(0.8629)	(1.1120)	(0.3729)	(0.4834)
Odr	2.2985*	0.7855	3.0711***	1.4101*
	(1.2511)	(1.7276)	(0.5436)	(0.7638)
Sr	2.6026***	2.8880***	−0.0324	−0.378
	(0.6763)	(1.1034)	(0.3559)	(0.9087)
Fs	−0.5747***	−0.6600***	−0.0707	−0.1581**
	(0.1682)	(0.2452)	(0.0525)	(0.0684)
Pms	−3.8834	−7.9448	−1.1434	−1.5699
	(4.5805)	(7.4640)	(1.8573)	(3.3501)
Control variables	controlled	controlled	controlled	controlled
_Cons	−0.8723	−0.413	0.2567	1.0479
	(1.0567)	(1.5036)	(0.4864)	(1.0179)
Obs	88	77	160	140
R2	0.3678	0.3215	0.7133	0.6657

Note: Values in parentheses are t-values. ***, **, and * denote significance at the 1%, 5%, and 10% confidence levels, respectively

Robustness Test

To ensure the robustness of the estimation results, this paper employs variable substitution and sample size variation methods to test the robustness of the results. First, the core explanatory variables are replaced. Specifically, the child dependency ratio and the old-age dependency ratio are substituted with the sampling ratio of the population under 14 years old and the sampling ratio of the population over 65 years old, respectively. Second, the estimation excludes the extremely large and small values of the household debt gap, constituting 1% of the full sample. The estimation results are presented in Table 5. The signs of the demographic structure variables are consistent with the previous estimation, and the magnitude of the coefficients does not change significantly, indicating that the results of this paper are robust.

Table 5. Results of Robustness Test

Variables	(1)	(2)
Sampling Ratio of Population Under 14 Years Old	0.6014	
	(1.9401)	
Sampling Ratio of Population Over 65 Years Old	9.7430***	
	(1.0546)	
Cdr		0.682
		(0.8826)
Odr		5.4939***
		(0.6516)
Sr	0.4741	0.5948
	(0.4008)	(0.3683)
Fs	−0.003	−0.0456
	(0.1320)	(0.0769)
Pms	−6.2964**	−4.3758**
	(2.5065)	(2.0483)
Control variables	controlled	controlled
_Cons	−0.6917	−0.5729
	(0.7744)	(0.6164)
Obs	217	248
R2	0.4788	0.5700

Note: Values in parentheses are t-values. ***, **, and * denote significance at the 1%, 5%, and 10% confidence levels, respectively

4.3 Mediating Effects of House Prices

The mediating effect of house prices on the relationship between the child dependency ratio and the household debt gap is presented in Table 6. In both the static panel model and the system GMM model, the effect of the child dependency ratio on house prices is significantly positive, as is the effect of house prices on the household debt gap. The z-statistics of Sobel's test are 4.712 and 8.3985, respectively, and are significant at the 1% level. This phenomenon can be explained by the fact that the increase in the number of children may temporarily impact house prices, but it does not affect house prices in core areas. Specifically, the rise in the child population drives the demand for quality education resources, which in turn increases the price of housing in school districts. The soaring prices of school district housing have become a powerful driver of overall house price increases, further exacerbating the problem of debt sustainability in the household. Thus, the estimation results in this paper confirm the transmission path of "child dependency ratio → house prices → household debt gap."

Table 6. Estimates of The Impact of House Prices on The Child Dependency Ratio on The Household Debt Gap

Variables	Static Panel			System GMM		
	Debt gap	lnhp	Debt gap	Debt gap	lnhp	Debt gap
L.Dg				0.4902***		0.0222
				(0.0265)		(0.0200)
L.Lnhp					0.9146***	
					(0.0250)	
Cdr	4.2318***	4.5363***	1.2217*	2.3367***	1.7374***	1.5736***
	(0.8970)	(0.8939)	(0.7151)	(0.1819)	(0.1909)	(0.2307)
Lnhp			0.6635***			0.6496***
			(0.0523)			(0.0298)
Sr	0.1536	0.0372	0.1289	1.1049***	0.4368***	0.8372***
	(0.4215)	(0.4200)	(0.3170)	(0.1990)	(0.1365)	(0.1315)
Fs	−0.1952**	−0.3021***	0.0053	−0.0656**	0.0226	0.0261
	(0.0865)	(0.0862)	(0.0669)	(0.0329)	(0.0241)	(0.0243)
Psm	−7.8428***	−7.5619***	−2.8251	−1.7100**	−3.8363***	−0.636
	(2.3202)	(2.3122)	(1.7891)	(0.8164)	(1.4034)	(1.2453)
Control variables	controlled	controlled	controlled	controlled	controlled	controlled
_Cons	0.7874	10.0958***	-5.9116***	−0.8206***	−0.1117	−6.4809***
	(0.6879)	(0.6855)	(0.7393)	(0.2569)	(0.3476)	(0.3892)

(*continued*)

Table 6. (*continued*)

Variables	Static Panel			System GMM		
	Debt gap	lnhp	Debt gap	Debt gap	lnhp	Debt gap
Obs	248	248	248	186	186	186
Sargan				0.1623	0.3310	0.0974
AR(1)				0.0990	0.0785	0.1020
AR(2)				0.2151	0.3257	0.2215
Mediation effects		3.0100			0.7631	
SobelZ		4.712***			8.3985***	

Note: Values in parentheses are t-values. ***, **, and * denote significance at the 1%, 5%, and 10% confidence levels, respectively

The mediating effect of house prices on the relationship between the old-age dependency ratio and the household debt gap is presented in Table 7. In both the static panel model and the system GMM model, the effect of the old-age dependency ratio on house prices is significantly positive, and the effect of house prices on the household debt gap is also significantly positive. The z-statistics of Sobel's test are 7.154 and 5.2582, respectively, and are significant at the 1% level. This suggests that China is in the early stages of aging, and the saving motivation of elderly parents, or the "altruistic" motivation to help their children buy a house, is driving the rise in house prices, which also exacerbates the problem of the sustainability of household debt. Thus, the estimation results of this paper verify the transmission path of "old-age dependency ratio → house prices → household debt gap." Assumption H4 holds.

Table 7. Estimates of The Impact of House Prices on The Old-age Dependency Ratio on The Household Debt Gap

Variables	Static Panel			System GMM		
	Debt gap	lnhp	Debt gap	Debt gap	lnhp	Debt gap
L.Dg				0.2437***		0.0795***
				(0.0150)		(0.0196)
L.Lnhp					0.8189***	
					(0.0295)	
Odr	5.7341***	6.5603***	2.0555***	7.1674***	1.7697***	4.1427***
	(0.5721)	(0.5314)	(0.6444)	(0.1689)	(0.2902)	(0.3303)
Lnhp			0.5607***			0.3696***

(*continued*)

Table 7. (*continued*)

Variables	Static Panel			System GMM		
	Debt gap	lnhp	Debt gap	Debt gap	lnhp	Debt gap
			(0.0639)			(0.0356)
Sr	0.5639	0.5357	0.2635	2.7269***	0.2733**	2.1006***
	(0.3657)	(0.3397)	(0.3148)	(0.1774)	(0.1116)	(0.1778)
Fs	−0.0505	−0.1299*	0.0224	−0.0077	−0.0046	−0.0207
	(0.0765)	(0.0711)	(0.0660)	(0.0326)	(0.0216)	(0.0202)
Pms	−4.2722**	−3.4491*	−2.3382	−6.8978***	−4.0216***	−5.3066***
	(2.0419)	(1.8968)	(1.7611)	(0.7874)	(1.1018)	(1.0802)
Control variables	controlled	controlled	controlled	controlled	controlled	controlled
_Cons	−0.3772	8.6155***	−5.2082***	−4.1872***	0.8810**	−6.1562***
	(0.5614)	(0.5215)	(0.7305)	(0.1963)	(0.3536)	(0.5065)
Obs	248	248	248	186	186	186
Sargan				0.2873	0.1957	0.1599
AR(1)				0.0757	0.0776	0.0859
AR(2)				0.4246	0.2597	0.3419
Mediation effects		3.6786			3.0247	
SobelZ		7.154***			5.2582***	

5 Conclusions

This paper investigates the impact of demographic structure on the sustainability of household liabilities using panel data from 31 provinces, cities, and autonomous regions in China from 2013 to 2020. The findings reveal that the child-rearing ratio and the old-age dependency ratio both have a positive effect on the sustainability of household liabilities, with these effects becoming more pronounced over time. There are significant regional differences between the eastern and central-western regions, and the total dependency ratio's impact on household indebtedness depends on the combined effects of the child and old-age dependency ratios. The sex ratio of the population exhibits a significant positive influence on household liabilities in the full sample and the eastern region, but has a non-significant effect in the central and western regions. Family size and population migration rate do not significantly affect the sustainability of household debt. Among the control variables, the income ratio of home purchase expenditure, the income ratio of consumption expenditure, and the GDP per capita growth rate show a facilitating effect on household liabilities, while the income ratio of financial security has a suppressing effect. The analysis further confirms that house prices play a mediating role in the relationship between demographic changes and the sustainability of household liabilities, with changes in the age structure of the population leading to increased household liabilities through rising house prices. Based on these empirical findings, several policy recommendations are proposed. These include liberalizing population fertility policies to increase family willingness to have children and mitigate China's aging population, and establishing a comprehensive preferential welfare system for families with multiple children to alleviate their financial burden. The government should also develop a job market for the elderly and provide re-employment opportunities for those over 60, which will ease the pressure on government pension payments and reduce the financial burden on families supporting elderly members. Enhancing the social security system for education and medical care by increasing special deductions for children's education and serious illness medical treatments is also recommended to alleviate families' financial burdens. Finally, implementing a comprehensive property tax system to curb "property speculation" and stabilize high housing prices, along with increasing the construction of public rental housing and low-cost housing to address the housing needs of low- and middle-income groups, will reduce families' debt burdens. These policy recommendations aim to address the underlying demographic and economic factors affecting the sustainability of household liabilities in China, promoting a more balanced and resilient economic structure.

Acknowledgement. The research of Lei Yu, Wenxian Zhou, Yujie Lin, Xinlong Yang and Jue Wang is supported by the grant of The MOE (Ministry of Education in China) Liberal Arts and Social Sciences Foundation "A study on the effect of intergenerational support on household debt behavior – a perspective based on life cycle theory" [NO. 18XJC790019], and Shenzhen Institute of Information Technology research start-up foundation "Research on the investment management mode of China's pension funds" [NO. SZIIT2021SK041].

References

Baltagi, B.H.: Panel Data Econometrics: Theoretical Contributions and Empirical Applications. Emerald Group Publishing (2006)

Campbell, J.Y., Cocco, J.F.: Household risk management and optimal mortgage choice. Quart. J. Econ. **118**(04), 1449–1494 (2003)

Campbell, J.Y., Cocco, J.F.: How do house prices affect consumption? Evidence from micro data. J. Monet. Econ. **54**(3), 591–621 (2007)

Chen, B., Li, T.: Urban household's assets and liabilities in China: facts and causes. Econ. Res. J. **46**(S1), 55–66+79 (2011). (in Chinese)

Crook, J.: The demand for household debt in the USA: evidence from the 1995 survey of consumer finance. Appl. Financ. Econ. **11**(01), 83–91 (2001)

Fabbri, D., Padula, M.: Does poor legal enforcement make households credit-constrained? J. Bank. Finance **28**(10), 2369–2397 (2004)

Hu, Z., Yang, H., Zang, R.: Household debt heterogeneity and analysis of influencing factors: microeconomic evidence in China. J. Bus. Econ. (09), 67–75 (2015)

Guo, X., Chen, B., Wu, Z.: An empirical study on the relationship between demographic changes and household debt growth in China. Stat. Decis. (04), 96–99 (2015). (in Chinese)

Igan, M.D., Loungani, M.P.: Global Housing Cycles. IMF Working Paper WP/12/217 (2012)

Jianakoplos, N.A., Bernasek, A.: Are women more risk averse? Econ. Inq. **36**(04), 620–630 (1998)

Lang, Y., Shen, B., Shi, Y., Ye, J.: Urban population migration, housing supply-demand equilibrium, and housing prices: a grouped empirical analysis based on purchase and loan restriction policies. Urban Probl. (01), 75–85 (2022). (in Chinese)

Li, L., Wu, X.: The consequences of having a son on family wealth in urban China. Rev. Income Wealth **63**(2), 378–393 (2017)

Liu, X., Zhou, H.: The influence of household individual characteristics on borrowing behavior: empirical evidence from Chinese households. J. Finan. Res. (10), 154–166 (2012). (in Chinese)

Liu, Z., Wang, Z., Chen, X.: The nonlinear effects of population aging on household debt. Econ. Perspect. (04), 64–78 (2020). (in Chinese)

Liu, Z., Pang, L., Chen, G.: The impact of demographic structure on household savings rates: based on provincial panel data from 1990–2018. World Surv. Res. (06), 38–49 (2021). (in Chinese)

Ruan, J., Liu, X., Ye, H.: A study on the current situation and influencing factors of the household leverage ratio in China. J. Finan. Res. (8), 18–33 (2020)

Shao, X., Wu, W., Huang, Y.: Population aging, house purchasing expenditure and the debt sustainability of household sector. J. Yunnan Univ. Finan. Econ. **34**(10), 52–61 (2018). (in Chinese)

Song, Q., Wu, Y., Yin, Z.: Financial literacy and household borrowing behavior. J. Finan. Res. (06), 95–110 (2017). (in Chinese)

Tong, W., Zhang, J.: A study on the influence of population aging and the real estate price fluctuation on the risk of residents' debt. Collected Essays Finan. Econ. (03), 19–28 (2018). (in Chinese)

Wang, S., Tian, X., Zhou, Y.: The trade-off between the quantity and quality of children in household fertility decisions: a review of the one-child policy. Lanzhou Acad. J. (06), 151–164 (2020). (in Chinese)

Worthington, A.C.: Debt as a source of financial stress in Australian households. Int. J. Consum. Stud. **30**(01), 2–15 (2006)

Wu, Z., Zhang, X.: Income inequality and changes in household debt in the view of urbanization: data from 30 provinces and cities. Econ. Manage. 30(03), 39–45 (2016). (in Chinese)

Xu, L., Zhou, J., Shi, Y.: Local fiscal pressure, land finance and housing prices. China Rev. Polit. Econ. **11**(04), 111–133 (2020). (in Chinese)

Yang, P., Zhu, F.: An empirical study on the impact of dependency ratio on consumer credit. Stat. Decis. (22), 165–168 (2016). (in Chinese)

Zhou, G., Wang, Y.: Housing prices, housing demand, and the debt ratio of Chinese households. J. Finan. Res. (06), 1–19 (2019). (in Chinese)

Zhou, L., Wang, C.: Population structure and household debt: microcosmic evidence from CFPS. Econ. Manage. **31**(03), 31–37 (2017). (in Chinese)

Zhu, W., Xia, Y.: An analysis on household consumption-fueled borrowing in China. J. Finan. Econ. **44**(10), 67–81 (2018). (in Chinese)

Evaluating Blockchain Platforms for Efficient Intellectual Property Rights Management: A Cross-Chain Analysis

P. H. T. Trung[1], D. M. Hieu[1(✉)], T. D. Khoa[1], H. G. Khiem[1], T. Q. Bao[1], T. N. Anh[1], V. C. P. Loc[1], and N. T. K. Ngan[2]

[1] FPT University, Can Tho city, Vietnam
trungpht@fe.edu.vn, hieudmce160738@fpt.edu.vn
[2] FPT Polytechnic, Can Tho city, Vietnam

Abstract. This paper examines the application of blockchain technology, smart contracts, and Non-Fungible Tokens (NFTs) in the management of intellectual property (IP) rights. We analyze four EVM-compatible blockchain platforms - BNB Chain, Fantom, Polygon, and Celo - to assess their suitability for IP management tasks. The study focuses on key operational aspects including transaction fees, gas limits, gas usage, and gas prices for common IP-related operations such as contract creation, NFT minting, and NFT transfer. By comparing these factors across platforms, we aim to provide insights into the economic feasibility and efficiency of blockchain-based IP management systems. Our findings reveal significant variations in cost structures and resource allocation among the platforms, which have important implications for their practical application in IP rights management. This research contributes to the ongoing discussion on the potential of blockchain technology to enhance the transparency, security, and efficiency of IP management processes in the digital age.

Keywords: Blockchain · Intellectual Property · NFTs · Smart Contracts · Cross-Chain Analysis

1 Introduction

The management of intellectual property (IP) rights has become increasingly complex in the digital age, challenging traditional systems and necessitating innovative solutions. This paper examines the potential of blockchain technology, smart contracts, and Non-Fungible Tokens (NFTs) to address these challenges, with a focus on enhancing transparency and efficiency in IP management processes across multiple blockchain platforms.

Conventional IP management systems, often centralized and bureaucratic, face numerous challenges in the digital era. These include difficulties in verifying ownership, combating piracy, and preventing unauthorized use of intellectual assets [9,16]. The traditional approach involves a linear process from creation

J. Zeng and L.-J. Zhang (Eds.): EDGE 2024, LNCS 15424, pp. 33–48, 2025.
https://doi.org/10.1007/978-3-031-77069-2_3

to registration and utilization, with intellectual property management agencies acting as intermediaries. However, this system can be slow, opaque, and prone to disputes. Blockchain technology offers a decentralized alternative [1,3], providing an immutable and transparent record of IP transactions that could potentially mitigate these issues.

The application of blockchain in IP management presents opportunities for streamlining rights assertion, licensing, and enforcement. Its decentralized nature facilitates the automation of IP transactions through smart contracts, potentially reducing intermediary involvement and associated costs [11,15]. The introduction of NFTs further enhances this ecosystem by enabling unique digital representations of IP rights, each with a clear ownership record. Smart contracts can automate various aspects of IP management, from licensing agreements to copyright enforcement, potentially simplifying the complex legal landscape surrounding intellectual property [4,5].

Our proposed blockchain-based IP management system integrates several key components. At its core is a user interface/user experience (UI/UX) system that serves as a central hub for interactions between creators, IP management agencies, and consumers. This system is synchronized with a distributed ledger, enhancing the security and traceability of IP records. Smart contracts facilitate the creation of NFTs representing intellectual property, which are then recorded on the blockchain. This approach aims to modernize IP management by combining traditional registration processes with emerging technologies, potentially offering enhanced efficiency, security, and accessibility for all stakeholders.

A key consideration in implementing blockchain-based IP management systems is economic feasibility. This study examines transaction fees for operations such as data creation, NFT minting, and NFT transfer across four EVM-compatible platforms: BNB Chain, Fantom, Polygon, and Celo [17]. Each platform presents distinct fee structures that influence its suitability for IP management. Our analysis covers critical factors such as transaction fees, gas limits, gas usage, and gas prices. These elements directly impact the cost and efficiency of performing IP-related operations on the blockchain and can significantly influence the choice of platform for implementing IP management solutions.

By examining the integration of blockchain and NFTs across multiple platforms, this research aims to provide stakeholders with a comprehensive understanding of how these technologies can be leveraged to create a more transparent, efficient, and secure framework for global IP management. We evaluate the strengths and limitations of each platform in the context of IP rights management, considering factors such as cost-effectiveness, resource allocation, and overall efficiency. This comparative approach allows us to assess which blockchain environments are best suited for various IP management tasks, ultimately guiding users and developers towards the most appropriate choices for their specific needs. The study contributes to the ongoing discourse on blockchain's potential to enhance IP rights management, offering a balanced assessment of the opportunities and challenges presented by these emerging technologies in the realm of intellectual property protection and management.

2   Related Work

2.1   Blockchain Applications in IP Rights Management

The integration of blockchain technology into IP rights management has been a subject of growing interest in recent years. Several researchers have explored how blockchain can enhance the security, transparency, and efficiency of IP management systems. Kumar and Tripathi examined blockchain's potential to create tamper-resistant records of IP rights, which could improve the overall transparency of the IP ecosystem [13]. Building on this concept, Finck and Moscon investigated how blockchain technology might influence copyright law, suggesting new approaches to rights administration [6]. In the realm of digital content distribution, Kishigami et al. proposed a blockchain-based system that could potentially streamline the process of managing and distributing copyrighted digital content [11]. This approach was further developed by Halloush and Yaseen, who presented a blockchain model aimed at preserving the integrity and transparency of intellectual property [9].

Researchers have also explored combining blockchain with other technologies to enhance IP protection. Meng et al. investigated the integration of digital watermarking with blockchain to improve the security of copyright management systems [16]. Similarly, Lin et al. proposed an architecture that leverages both blockchain and IoT technologies to protect intellectual property [15]. The concept of decentralized file systems has also been explored in the context of IP management. Benet introduced the IPFS, a peer-to-peer network that could potentially support IP management by ensuring content integrity and accessibility [2]. Rambhia et al. provided an overview of how blockchain technology could enhance the transparency and operational efficiency of IP rights management systems [18].

Recent studies have further expanded on these concepts. Ferro et al. examined the use of smart legal contracts on blockchain platforms for managing digital asset rights [4]. The potential of blockchain and smart contracts in redefining intellectual property management was discussed by Fidalgo in the context of international law [5]. Lando and Miashchanava explored how blockchain could strengthen IP rights, presenting their findings at an economic systems conference [14]. The legal implications of using distributed ledger technology for IP rights management were analyzed by Hauck, who advocated for adapting traditional legal frameworks to accommodate these new technologies [10]. Building on this, Rambhia and colleagues proposed a blockchain-based model for IP management, discussing both design and implementation strategies [19].

2.2   Legal Considerations in Digital IP Rights Management

The evolution of intellectual property laws in response to digital technologies, particularly blockchain, has been a topic of significant academic discourse. Singh examined the challenges faced by copyright and patent protection in light of technological advancements [20]. Ferro et al. further explored the application of smart legal contracts and blockchain technology in managing digital asset rights [4]. The intersection of intellectual property law and blockchain technology was analyzed by Gürkaynak et al., who considered the implications for existing legal frameworks [8]. Kraus and Boulay delved into the legal challenges and potential solutions in intellectual property law as they relate to blockchain technology [12]. Finck and Moscon discussed the adaptation of copyright law to blockchain platforms, highlighting a shift towards decentralized rights administration [7]. These studies collectively emphasize the need for legal systems to evolve in order to accommodate the enhanced transparency and management capabilities offered by blockchain, NFTs, and smart contracts in the domain of intellectual property rights.

3   Approach

3.1   Traditional Approach for Intellectual Property Rights Management

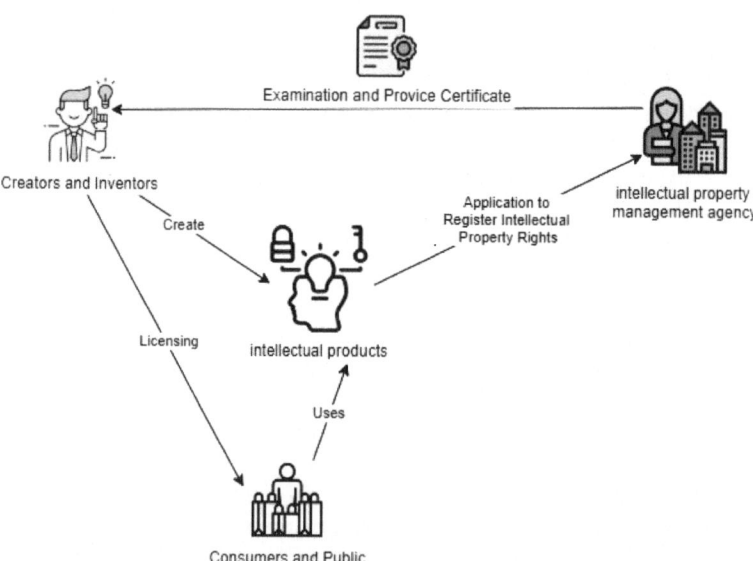

Fig. 1. Process Flow of Intellectual Property Rights Management

Figure 1 illustrates the lifecycle and key stakeholders involved in the creation, protection, and utilization of intellectual property. It depicts a comprehensive process that begins with creators and inventors, progresses through the development and registration of intellectual products, and culminates in their use by consumers and the public. At the origin of this process are the creators and inventors, represented by an icon of a person with a lightbulb, symbolizing the generation of ideas. These individuals are the source of intellectual products, which can take various forms such as inventions, artistic works, or brand identities. The creators develop these intellectual products, represented in the diagram by a stylized head containing a lightbulb, gears, and a lock, suggesting the mental processes and protective nature of these creations.

Once intellectual products are developed, creators have the option to seek formal protection for their work. This is shown by the arrow pointing from the intellectual products to the intellectual property management agency, depicted as a figure next to buildings, implying an official or governmental body. The arrow is labeled "Application to Register Intellectual Property Rights," indicating the formal process creators must undertake to secure legal protection for their work. The agency then conducts an examination of the application and, if approved, issues a certificate, as shown by the arrow flowing back to the creators labeled "Examination and Provide Certificate."

The diagram also illustrates two primary paths for the utilization of intellectual products. One path leads directly to consumers and the public, represented by a group of figures at the bottom of the image. This suggests that some intellectual products may be used or consumed directly by the public without intermediaries. The other path involves licensing, as indicated by an arrow pointing from the creators to the consumers and public. Licensing allows creators to grant permission for others to use their intellectual property under specific terms and conditions, potentially generating revenue while maintaining ownership rights.

The overall structure of the diagram emphasizes the interconnected nature of intellectual property systems. It shows how ideas flow from creation to protection, and then to use by the public, with various stakeholders and processes involved at each stage. This representation provides a basic framework for understanding the ecosystem of intellectual property rights, highlighting the roles of creators, regulatory bodies, and end-users in the lifecycle of intellectual products.

3.2   Blockchain-Based Intellectual Property Management System

Figure 2 presents a comprehensive overview of an intellectual property (IP) management system that incorporates blockchain technology. This system outlines the process from the creation of intellectual products to their registration, management, and public interaction, with the addition of smart contracts and distributed ledger technology. At the beginning of the process, creators and inventors are depicted, symbolized by a figure with a lightbulb, indicating the generation of ideas. These individuals create intellectual products, represented by an icon showing a head with various symbols inside, suggesting the diverse nature of intellectual creations. The arrow labeled "Create" connects these two elements, representing the act of bringing ideas into tangible or intangible forms that can be protected as intellectual property.

Once intellectual products are created, the diagram shows two primary pathways. The first involves applying for official registration of intellectual property rights. This is illustrated by an arrow pointing from the intellectual products

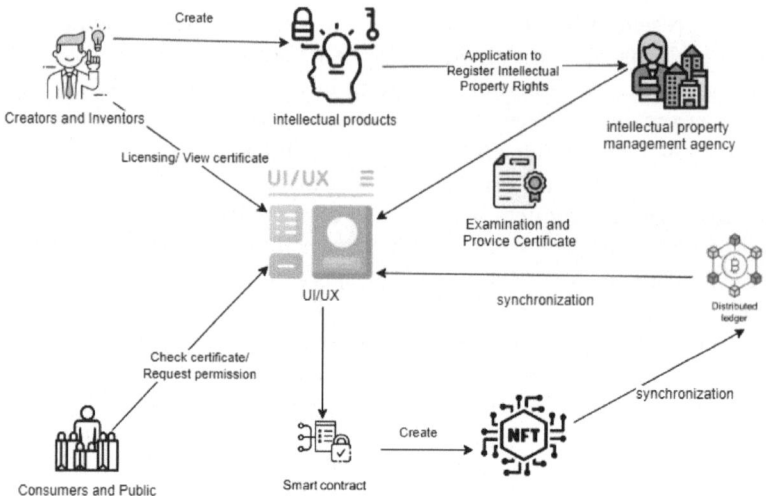

Fig. 2. Intellectual Property Management System with Blockchain Integration

to the intellectual property management agency, represented by a figure next to buildings. This agency is responsible for examining applications and issuing certificates, as indicated by the arrow flowing back labeled "Examination and Provide Certificate." The second pathway involves the integration of the intellectual property into a user interface or user experience (UI/UX) system. This UI/UX component appears to be central to the entire process, serving as a hub for various interactions. It receives input from multiple sources: the licensing and viewing of certificates from creators, examination results from the IP management agency, and interactions with consumers and the public.

A notable addition to this system is the incorporation of blockchain technology, represented by the "Distributed ledger" icon. The blockchain is connected to the UI/UX system through a bidirectional "synchronization" arrow, suggesting that information is regularly updated and verified between the user interface and the distributed ledger. This integration likely aims to enhance the security, transparency, and traceability of intellectual property records and transactions.

The diagram also introduces the concept of smart contracts, depicted as a document with a checkmark. These smart contracts are shown creating NFTs, which are also synchronized with the distributed ledger. This suggests a system where intellectual property can be tokenized, potentially allowing for more efficient management, trading, or licensing of IP rights through blockchain technology. Lastly, the figure shows how consumers and the public interact with this system. They can check certificates or request permissions through the UI/UX interface, indicating a streamlined process for verifying and accessing intellectual property information. This comprehensive system appears designed to modernize IP management by combining traditional registration processes with emerging technologies, potentially offering enhanced efficiency, security, and accessibility for all stakeholders involved in the intellectual property ecosystem.

4   Evaluation Scenarios

In the evaluation section, we focus on cross-chain functionality for Intellectual Property Rights Management, specifically examining four EVM-supported platformsEthereum Virtual Machine (EVM), including Binance Smart Chain (BNB Smart Chain)[1]; Polygon[2]; Fantom[3]; and Celo[4]. The decision to consider multiple platforms stems from the need to identify the most suitable environment for implementing and managing intellectual property rights in a blockchain context. Each platform offers unique characteristics and trade-offs, which can significantly impact the efficiency and cost-effectiveness of intellectual property management processes.

By analyzing several platforms, we aim to provide a comprehensive understanding of how different blockchain environments handle intellectual property-related transactions. This comparative approach allows us to assess the strengths and limitations of each platform in the context of intellectual property rights management, ultimately guiding users and developers towards the most appropriate choice for their specific needs. Our analysis centers on three primary methods crucial to intellectual property management on blockchain: transaction creation, NFT minting, and NFT transfer. These operations represent key processes in the lifecycle of digital intellectual property assets, from initial registration to ownership transfer. By examining these methods across different platforms, we can gauge the overall performance and suitability of each blockchain for intellectual property rights management tasks.

To conduct a thorough evaluation, we analyze several critical factors that influence the performance and cost-effectiveness of blockchain operations[5]. These factors include transaction fees, gas limits, gas used by transactions, and gas prices. Transaction fees are particularly important as they directly affect the cost of performing intellectual property-related operations on the blockchain. The gas limit and gas used by transactions provide insights into the computational resources required for these operations, which can impact transaction speed and network congestion. Gas prices, which can fluctuate based on network demand, play a significant role in determining the overall cost of transactions. It's worth noting that while burn fees are a factor in some blockchain ecosystems, particularly BNB and MATIC (Polygon), we have chosen not to include this in our analysis. This decision is based on the fact that burn fees are not universally implemented across all the platforms under consideration, and their impact on intellectual property management operations may be minimal or indirect.

By examining these factors across BNB, Fantom, Polygon, and Celo, we aim to provide a nuanced understanding of how each platform performs in the context of intellectual property rights management. This analysis will help stakeholders make informed decisions about which blockchain environment best suits their

---

[1] https://github.com/bnb-chain/whitepaper/blob/master/WHITEPAPER.md.

[2] https://polygon.technology/lightpaper-polygon.pdf.

[3] https://whitepaper.io/document/438/fantom-whitepaper.

[4] https://celo.org/papers/whitepaper.

[5] Time of evaluation: 11:00AM - GMT+7 - August 10th 2024.

needs for managing digital intellectual property assets. The results of this evaluation will offer valuable insights into the trade-offs between transaction costs, processing speed, and overall efficiency across these different blockchain platforms.

4.1   Transaction Fee

Table 1. Transaction fee

	Contract Creation	Create NFT	Transfer NFT
BNB Smart Chain	0.0273134 BNB ($13.91)	0.00109162 BNB ($0.56)	0.00057003 BNB ($0.29)
Fantom	0.00957754 FTM ($0.00)	0.000405167 FTM ($0.00)	0.0002380105 FTM ($0.00)
Polygon	0.006840710032835408 MATIC ($0.01)	0.000289405001852192 MATIC ($0.00)	0.000170007501088048 MATIC ($0.00)
Celo	0.007097844 CELO ($0.003)	0.0002840812 CELO ($0.000)	0.0001554878 CELO ($0.000)

The analysis of transaction fees across the four EVM-supported platforms, is presented in Table 1, reveals significant variations in cost structure for intellectual property rights management operations. These differences can substantially impact the choice of platform for implementing IP-related blockchain solutions. BNB Smart Chain exhibits the highest transaction fees among the four platforms. Contract creation on BNB Smart Chain costs 0.0273134 BNB, equivalent to approximately $13.91, which is notably higher than the other networks. NFT creation and transfer operations on BNB Smart Chain are also more expensive, at 0.00109162 BNB ($0.56) and 0.00057003 BNB ($0.29) respectively. These higher fees could potentially deter users from utilizing BNB Smart Chain for frequent IP-related transactions, especially in scenarios involving numerous small-value operations. In contrast, Fantom demonstrates remarkably low transaction fees across all three operations. The costs for contract creation (0.00957754 FTM), NFT creation (0.000405167 FTM), and NFT transfer (0.0002380105 FTM) on Fantom are negligible when converted to USD, all rounding to $0.00. This cost-effectiveness could make Fantom an attractive option for users looking to minimize transaction expenses, particularly for high-volume IP management tasks.

Polygon presents a middle ground in terms of transaction fees. While its fees are higher than Fantom's, they remain very low when converted to USD. Contract creation on Polygon costs 0.006840710032835408 MATIC ($0.01), with NFT creation and transfer fees being even lower at 0.000289405001852192 MATIC and 0.000170007501088048 MATIC respectively, both rounding to $0.00 in USD. This balance of low fees and widespread adoption could make Polygon a practical choice for many IP management applications. Celo's fee structure is similar to Polygon's in terms of USD conversion, with all operations costing less than a cent. Contract creation on Celo costs 0.007097844 CELO ($0.003), NFT creation 0.0002840812 CELO, and NFT transfer 0.0001554878 CELO, with the latter two rounding to $0.000 in USD. This fee structure positions Celo as another cost-effective option for IP rights management on the blockchain.

The substantial difference in fees between BNB Smart Chain and the other networks underscores the importance of considering transaction costs in choosing a platform for IP rights management. While BNB Smart Chain may offer other advantages, its higher fees could be a significant factor for users planning frequent transactions or working with lower-value IP assets. Conversely, the extremely low fees on Fantom, Polygon, and Celo make these platforms potentially more suitable for applications requiring numerous transactions or dealing with smaller-scale IP assets. However, it's crucial to note that transaction fees should be considered alongside other factors such as network security, ecosystem support, and overall platform stability when making a final decision on which blockchain to use for IP rights management.

4.2 Gas Limit

Table 2. Gas limit

	Contract Creation	Create NFT	Transfer NFT
BNB Smart Chain	2,731,340	109,162	72,003
Fantom	2,736,440	115,762	72,803
Polygon	2,736,284	115,762	72,803
Celo	3,548,922	142,040	85,673

Table 2 analysis of gas limits across the four EVM-supported platforms reveals interesting patterns in resource allocation for intellectual property rights management operations. For contract creation, we observe that BNB Smart Chain, Fantom, and Polygon have relatively similar gas limits, ranging from 2,731,340 to 2,736,440 units. This similarity suggests a comparable approach to resource allocation for complex operations like deploying new smart contracts. However, Celo stands out with a significantly higher gas limit of 3,548,922 units for contract creation. This higher limit on Celo could potentially allow for more complex or feature-rich smart contracts to be deployed, which might be beneficial for sophisticated intellectual property management systems.

When it comes to creating NFTs, which is a key operation in tokenizing intellectual property, we see more variation among the platforms. BNB Smart Chain has the lowest gas limit at 109,162 units, while Fantom and Polygon both allocate 115,762 units. Celo again provides the highest gas limit at 142,040 units. These differences could impact the complexity and features of NFTs that can be minted on each platform, potentially affecting the richness of metadata or additional functionalities that can be incorporated into IP-related tokens. For NFT transfers, which represent ownership changes of intellectual property assets, the gas limits are more consistent across platforms, with slight variations. BNB Smart Chain has the lowest limit at 72,003 units, while Fantom and Polygon both allocate 72,803 units. Celo maintains its trend of higher limits with 85,673 units for NFT transfers. These differences, while less pronounced than in other operations, could still affect the efficiency and potential additional features of NFT transfers on each platform.

The consistently higher gas limits on Celo across all three operations suggest that this platform may be more accommodating to complex or resource-intensive operations in IP rights management. This could be advantageous for implementing advanced features or handling large-scale IP management systems. However, it's important to note that higher gas limits don't necessarily translate to better performance or lower costs, as other factors like network congestion and gas prices also play significant roles. The similarities in gas limits between Fantom and Polygon for NFT creation and transfer operations indicate that these platforms may offer comparable capabilities for standard IP management tasks. BNB Smart Chain's slightly lower limits might necessitate more efficient smart contract design to ensure operations fit within the allocated gas limits.

These gas limit variations across platforms highlight the need for developers and users to consider the specific requirements of their IP management applications when choosing a blockchain network. While higher gas limits provide more flexibility, they may also lead to higher costs if not managed efficiently. Conversely, lower gas limits might require more optimized code but could result in lower transaction costs. Balancing these factors alongside other considerations like transaction fees, network security, and ecosystem support is crucial for implementing effective blockchain-based intellectual property rights management systems.

4.3   Gas Used by Transaction

Table 3. Gas Used by Transaction

	Contract Creation	Create NFT	Transfer NFT
BNB Smart Chain	2,731,340 (100%)	109,162 (100%)	57,003 (79.17%)
Fantom	2,736,440 (100%)	115,762 (100%)	68,003 (93.41%)
Polygon	2,736,284 (100%)	115,762 (100%)	68,003 (93.41%)
Celo	2,729,940 (76.92%)	109,262 (76.92%)	59,803 (69.8%)

Table 3 presents gas used by transactions across the four EVM-supported platforms reveals insightful patterns in resource utilization for intellectual property rights management operations. For contract creation, we observe that BNB Smart Chain, Fantom, and Polygon all utilize 100% of their allocated gas limits. This full utilization suggests that these platforms have optimized their gas limits to closely match the typical requirements for deploying smart contracts related to IP management. Celo, however, stands out with a lower gas usage of 2,729,940 units, which represents only 76.92% of its higher gas limit. This lower utilization on Celo could indicate either more efficient contract deployment processes or potentially underutilized resources for this operation. In the case of NFT creation, a key operation for tokenizing intellectual property, we see a similar pattern. BNB Smart Chain, Fantom, and Polygon again use 100% of their allocated gas, indicating that their gas limits are well-calibrated for this operation. Celo maintains its trend of lower utilization, using 109,262 units of gas, which is 76.92% of its limit. This consistent pattern across contract creation and NFT minting on Celo might suggest a deliberate design choice to allow for more complex operations or future scalability.

The gas usage for NFT transfers shows more variation across platforms. BNB Smart Chain uses 57,003 units, representing 79.17% of its gas limit for this operation. Fantom and Polygon both use 68,003 units, which is 93.41% of their allocated gas. This high utilization on Fantom and Polygon suggests that their gas limits are more tightly optimized for NFT transfer operations. Celo uses 59,803 units, which is 69.8% of its limit, continuing its trend of lower gas utilization across all operations. These utilization patterns have several implications for intellectual property rights management on blockchain. The 100% utilization seen on BNB Smart Chain, Fantom, and Polygon for contract creation and NFT minting suggests that these platforms have calibrated their systems to closely match the needs of these operations. This could lead to more predictable transaction costs and efficient resource use. However, it also means that there's little room for additional complexity in these operations without increasing gas limits.

Celo's consistently lower gas utilization across all operations presents an interesting case. While it might suggest inefficiency at first glance, it could also indicate that Celo's infrastructure is designed to accommodate more complex or variable operations in IP management. This extra headroom could be beneficial for implementing advanced features or handling unexpected complexities in IP-related smart contracts. The variations in gas usage for NFT transfers are particularly noteworthy. The lower utilization on BNB Smart Chain and Celo compared to their contract creation and NFT minting operations might indicate that these platforms have optimized their systems for more efficient ownership transfers of IP assets. Conversely, the high utilization on Fantom and Polygon suggests that NFT transfers on these platforms are using nearly all available resources, which could potentially limit the inclusion of additional features in transfer operations.

These findings underscore the importance of considering gas utilization patterns when selecting a blockchain platform for IP rights management. While full utilization might indicate efficient resource allocation, it could also limit flexibility for more complex operations. Conversely, lower utilization might offer more room for advanced features but could potentially result in higher costs if gas limits are not adjusted accordingly. Balancing these factors alongside other considerations such as transaction fees and network characteristics is crucial for implementing effective and efficient blockchain-based intellectual property management systems.

Table 4. Gas Price

	Contract Creation	Create NFT	Transfer NFT
BNB Smart Chain	0.00000001 BNB (10 Gwei)	0.00000001 BNB (10 Gwei)	0.00000001 BNB (10 Gwei)
Fantom	0.0000000035 FTM (3.5 Gwei)	0.0000000035 FTM (3.5 Gwei)	0.0000000035 FTM (3.5 Gwei)
Polygon	0.000000002500000012 MATIC (2.500000012 Gwei)	0.000000002500000016 MATIC (2.500000016 Gwei)	0.000000002500000016 MATIC (2.500000016 Gwei)
Celo	0.0000000026 CELO (Max Fee per Gas: 2.7 Gwei)	0.0000000026 CELO (Max Fee per Gas: 2.7 Gwei)	0.0000000026 CELO (Max Fee per Gas: 2.7 Gwei)

4.4   Gas Price

The analysis of Table 4 presents the gas prices, revealing variations in the cost structure for executing intellectual property rights management operations on these blockchains. BNB Smart Chain demonstrates the highest gas price among the four platforms, with a consistent rate of 0.00000001 BNB (10 Gwei) across all three operations: contract creation, NFT creation, and NFT transfer. This uniformity in gas price simplifies cost calculations for users but also means that BNB Smart Chain maintains relatively higher transaction costs compared to the other networks examined. The higher gas price on BNB Smart Chain could potentially impact the frequency and scale of IP-related transactions, especially for operations involving numerous small-value assets or frequent updates. Fantom offers a significantly lower gas price at 0.0000000035 FTM (3.5 Gwei) for all three operations. This lower gas price could make Fantom an attractive option for users looking to minimize transaction costs in their IP management processes. The reduced costs might enable more frequent transactions or the handling of larger volumes of IP assets without incurring prohibitive fees. However, it's important to note that the actual cost in fiat currency would depend on the current exchange rate of FTM.

Polygon presents a slightly more complex gas price structure, with minor variations across operations. For contract creation, the gas price is 0.000000002500000012 MATIC (2.500000012 Gwei), while for NFT creation and transfer, it's 0.000000002500000016 MATIC (2.500000016 Gwei). These prices are lower than both BNB Smart Chain and Fantom, potentially making Polygon a cost-effective choice for IP management tasks. The slight difference in gas price between contract creation and NFT operations on Polygon is minimal and likely wouldn't significantly impact overall costs for most use cases. Celo employs a unique approach with its gas pricing mechanism. It uses a consistent price of 0.0000000026 CELO across all operations, but specifies this as a "Max Fee per Gas" of 2.7 Gwei. This structure suggests that Celo implements a form of dynamic gas pricing, where the actual gas price might fluctuate below this maximum value depending on network conditions. This approach could potentially offer users more predictable maximum costs while allowing for lower fees during periods of reduced network congestion.

The variations in gas prices across these platforms highlight the importance of considering transaction costs when selecting a blockchain for IP rights management. While BNB Smart Chain's higher gas prices might be offset by other advantages of its ecosystem, they could pose challenges for applications requiring high-frequency or low-value transactions. Fantom and Polygon's lower gas prices could make them more suitable for such scenarios, potentially enabling more granular or frequent IP management operations. Celo's approach of setting a maximum fee introduces an interesting dynamic, potentially offering a balance between cost predictability and efficiency. This could be particularly beneficial for IP management systems that require consistent budgeting while still taking advantage of potential cost savings during off-peak periods.

It's crucial to note that while gas prices are an important factor, they should be considered alongside other metrics such as transaction speed, network security, and ecosystem support when choosing a platform for IP rights management. Additionally, the volatile nature of cryptocurrency prices means that the fiat currency equivalent of these gas prices can fluctuate, adding another layer of consideration for long-term planning of blockchain-based IP management systems. Balancing these factors is essential for implementing a cost-effective and efficient intellectual property rights management solution on blockchain platforms.

5   Discussion

5.1   Cost Implications for IP Management

The analysis of transaction fees and gas prices across the four EVM-supported platforms reveals significant implications for the cost-effectiveness of intellectual property management on blockchain. BNB Smart Chain consistently demonstrates the highest costs, with transaction fees for contract creation reaching $13.91, substantially higher than its competitors. This cost structure may pose challenges for frequent or small-scale IP transactions, potentially limiting its suitability for certain types of IP management systems. In contrast, Fantom, Polygon, and Celo offer remarkably low transaction fees, with costs often rounding to $0.00 in USD for NFT creation and transfer operations. This cost-effectiveness could be particularly advantageous for IP management systems that require frequent transactions or deal with large volumes of low-value assets. The minimal fees on these platforms might encourage more granular tracking and management of intellectual property, potentially enabling new use cases that were previously cost-prohibitive. However, it's important to consider that the relative cost-effectiveness of these platforms may fluctuate with cryptocurrency market conditions. The volatility of token prices means that the fiat currency equivalent of transaction fees and gas prices can change rapidly, introducing an element of uncertainty for long-term planning. Organizations implementing IP management systems on blockchain must factor in this potential variability and may need to develop strategies to mitigate the impact of price fluctuations on their operations.

5.2   Resource Allocation and Efficiency

The examination of gas limits and gas usage patterns across the platforms provides insights into their resource allocation strategies and overall efficiency in handling IP-related operations. BNB Smart Chain, Fantom, and Polygon demonstrate high utilization rates, often using 100% of their allocated gas for contract creation and NFT minting. This suggests these platforms have optimized their systems to closely match the typical requirements of these operations, potentially leading to more predictable performance and resource usage.

Celo's approach stands out, with consistently lower gas utilization across all operations. While this could be interpreted as inefficiency, it may also indicate that Celo's infrastructure is designed to accommodate more complex or variable operations in IP management. This extra capacity could prove beneficial for implementing advanced features or handling unexpected complexities in IP-related smart contracts. However, it also raises questions about the potential for higher costs if this extra capacity is not effectively managed or utilized. The variations in gas usage for NFT transfers are particularly noteworthy. The lower utilization on BNB Smart Chain and Celo for this operation, compared to their contract creation and NFT minting operations, suggests these platforms may have optimized for efficient ownership transfers of IP assets. This could be advantageous for IP management systems that involve frequent transfers or trades of intellectual property rights.

5.3   Platform Selection Considerations

The evaluation results underscore the complexity of choosing the most suitable blockchain platform for IP rights management. While cost is a crucial factor, with Fantom, Polygon, and Celo offering significant advantages in terms of transaction fees and gas prices, it should not be the sole consideration. The higher costs associated with BNB Smart Chain might be justified by other factors such as ecosystem maturity, developer support, or integration with existing systems. The resource allocation patterns and efficiency metrics provide additional dimensions for consideration. Platforms with high gas utilization, like BNB Smart Chain, Fantom, and Polygon, may offer more predictable performance but could limit flexibility for implementing more complex IP management features. Celo's lower utilization rates might provide more room for advanced functionalities but could potentially result in higher costs if not managed efficiently. The unique approaches of each platform, such as Celo's maximum fee structure for gas prices, also merit consideration. These distinctive features may align better with specific IP management strategies or organizational requirements. For instance, Celo's approach might be particularly suitable for organizations that prioritize predictable maximum costs in their IP management operations.

Ultimately, the selection of a blockchain platform for IP rights management should involve a holistic assessment of an organization's specific needs, including the volume and frequency of IP-related transactions, the complexity of desired features, budget constraints, and long-term scalability requirements. The evaluation results provide a foundation for this assessment, but additional factors such as network security, ecosystem support, and compatibility with existing IP management processes should also be carefully weighed in the decision-making process.

6   Conclusion

Our analysis of BNB Chain, Fantom, Polygon, and Celo for intellectual property rights management reveals significant variations in their suitability for different IP-related tasks. Each platform offers distinct trade-offs between transaction costs, resource allocation, and operational efficiency. BNB Chain provides consistency but at higher costs, while Fantom and Polygon offer cost-effectiveness at the potential expense of complexity handling. Celo's unique approach balances flexibility with predictable pricing. These findings emphasize the importance of aligning platform selection with specific IP management needs. The choice of blockchain platform can substantially impact the economic viability and operational efficiency of IP management systems, particularly when considering factors such as transaction volume, complexity of operations, and budget constraints. While blockchain technology shows potential in addressing challenges in IP management, its implementation requires careful consideration of various factors beyond those examined in this study. As the technology and regulatory landscape evolve, continued research will be crucial to fully realize the benefits of blockchain in enhancing transparency, reducing disputes, and streamlining IP processes. Stakeholders must weigh these considerations carefully to effectively leverage blockchain technology in IP rights management.

References

1. Bang, N.H., et al.: Blockchain-enhanced IoHT: a patient-centric internet of health-care things platform with smart contract-driven data management. In: Delir Haghighi, P., Khalil, I., Kotsis, G., ER, N.A.S. (eds.) Advances in Mobile Computing and Multimedia Intelligence, MoMM 2023. LNCS, vol. 14417, pp. 50–56. Springer, Cham (2023). https://doi.org/10.1007/978-3-031-48348-6_4
2. Benet, J.: IPFS-content addressed, versioned, P2P file system. arxiv.org (2014)
3. Duong-Trung, N., et al.: Multi-sessions mechanism for decentralized cash on delivery system. Int. J. Adv. Comput. Sci. Appl. **10**(9), 553–560 (2019)
4. Ferro, E., et al.: Digital assets rights management through smart legal contracts and smart contracts. Blockchain Res. Appl. **4**(3), 100142 (2023)
5. Fidalgo, V.P.: Blockchain(s), smart contracts and intellectual property, pp. 295–319 (2022)
6. Finck, M., Moscon, V.: Copyright law on blockchains: between new forms of rights administration and digital rights management 2.0. IIC. International Review of Intellectual Property Competition Law (2018)
7. Finck, M., Moscon, V.: Copyright law on blockchains: between new forms of rights administration and digital rights management 2.0. IIC-International Review of Intellectual Property and Competition Law **50**, 77–108 (2019)
8. Gürkaynak, G., Yılmaz, I., Yeşilaltay, B., Bengi, B.: Intellectual property law and practice in the blockchain realm. Comput. Law Secur. Rev. **34**(4), 847–862 (2018)
9. Halloush, Z., Yaseen, Q.: A blockchain model for preserving intellectual property. In: Proceedings of the ACM Conference (2019)
10. Hauck, R.: Blockchain, smart contracts and intellectual property. using distributed ledger technology to protect, license and enforce intellectual property rights. Legal Issues in the Digital Age **1**(1), 17–41 (2021)

11. Kishigami, J., Fujimura, S., Watanabe, H., Nakadaira, A., Akutsu, A.: The blockchain-based digital content distribution system. In: 2015 IEEE Fifth International Conference on Big Data and Cloud Computing. IEEE (2015)
12. Kraus, D., Boulay, C.: Blockchains: aspects of intellectual property law. In: Blockchains, Smart Contracts, Decentralised Autonomous Organisations and the Law, pp. 240–271. Edward Elgar Publishing (2019)
13. Kumar, B., Tripathi, A.: Blockchain technology and intellectual property rights. nopr.niscair.res.in (2018)
14. Lando, D.D., Miashchanava, M.V.: Strengthening intellectual property rights and blockchain technology, pp. 1532–1540 (2021)
15. Lin, J., Long, W., Zhang, A., Chai, Y.: Blockchain and IoT-based architecture design for intellectual property protection. Int. J. Crowd Sci. **4**, 283–293 (2020)
16. Meng, Z., Morizumi, T., Miyata, S., Kinoshita, H.: Design scheme of copyright management system based on digital watermarking and blockchain. In: COMPSAC 2018. IEEE (2018)
17. Quoc, K.L., et al.: SSSB: an approach to insurance for cross-border exchange by using smart contracts. In: Awan, I., Younas, M., Poniszewska-Marańda, A. (eds.) Mobile Web and Intelligent Information Systems, MobiWIS 2022. LNCS, vol. 13475, pp. 179–192. Springer, Cham (2022). https://doi.org/10.1007/978-3-031-14391-5_14
18. Rambhia, V., Mehta, V., Mehta, R., Shah, R., Patel, D.: Intellectual property rights management using blockchain. In: Kaiser, M.S., Xie, J., Rathore, V.S. (eds.) Information and Communication Technology for Competitive Strategies (ICTCS 2020). LNNS, vol. 190, pp. 545–552. Springer, Singapore (2021). https://doi.org/10.1007/978-981-16-0882-7_47
19. Rambhia, V., Mehta, V., Mehta, R., Shah, R., Patel, D.: Intellectual property rights management using blockchain, pp. 545–552 (2021)
20. Singh, G.: Intellectual property rights in the digital age: challenges and solutions for copyright and patent protection. Int. J. Adv. Res. Manage. Soc. Sci. **5**, 143–150 (2016)

Design and Implementation of HPLC and HRF Dual Mode Standard Transceiver Unit

Lin Pang[✉], Jinyu Zhao, Zhidan Lan, Chao Peng, Zhihui Liu, and Yangyang Ge

China Gridcom Co., Ltd, Shenzhen 518110, Guangdong, China

Abstract. With the continuous upgrading of communication technology in low-voltage distribution network, dual-mode communication combining high speed power line carrier (HPLC) and high speed wireless communication (HRF) has become the most critical communication technology in the field of low-voltage power grid. This paper deeply studies the interworking technology of dual-mode communication, analyzes the detection scheme of dual-mode communication, and designs a dual-mode standard transceiver unit. To realize the data interaction with the user platform system, analyze and convert the platform data message into MPDU frame, realize the processing functions of carrier or wireless MPDU frame analysis, coding, modulation, etc., and carry out simulation verification to realize the protocol consistency test of dual-mode communication unit.

Keywords: Low voltage power grid · High speed power line communication · High speed radio frequency · Field programmable gate array

1 Introduction

In recent years, with the continuous advancement of digital and intelligent construction of low-voltage power grids, new power systems have emerged [1, 2]. High Speed Power Line Communication (HPLC) has become the preferred technology for the construction of new power systems. It adopts Orthogonal Frequency Division Multiplexing (OFDM) technology, which has the characteristics of high reliability, large bandwidth and high speed. However, HPLC communication relies heavily on the reliability of power lines, and cannot access non-power line powered equipment, which cannot meet the needs of communication services in some specific scenarios. High Speed Radio Frequency (HRF) uses the wireless channel as the communication medium, which is not affected by factors such as power lines, and can effectively complement HPLC technology [3–5]. Dual-mode communication technology integrates HPLC and HRF two communication technologies. Based on the link layer protocol of HPLC, the HRF channel network routing mechanism is added to enable dual-channel automatic fusion networking, which can be oriented to more diversified business scenarios. In addition, in dual-mode technology, the two channels can be alternate paths to each other to further ensure the reliability of communication and services [6–8].

With the rise of dual-mode communication technology, the detection capability of dual-mode communication is particularly important [9]. In this paper, the interconnection

J. Zeng and L.-J. Zhang (Eds.): EDGE 2024, LNCS 15424, pp. 49–58, 2025.
https://doi.org/10.1007/978-3-031-77069-2_4

technology of dual-mode communication is deeply studied, and a dual-mode standard transceiver unit is designed and implemented. The transceiver unit is mainly composed of a transparent transmitter and a transparent receiver. The transceiver unit can exchange data with the user platform and convert the interactive data into MPDU frames. At the same time, the MPDU frame can be encoded and modulated, converted into physical layer data unit and sent to the dual-mode channel to realize the protocol consistency test of the dual-mode communication unit.

2 Dual-Mode Standard Transceiver Unit Overall Structure Design

The overall design structure of the dual-mode standard transceiver unit realized in this paper is shown in Fig. 1. The upper computer software platform sends the assembled data packets to the ARM processing unit through the Ethernet interface, and analyzes the data packets returned by the ARM processing unit at the same time. The main functions of the ARM processing unit are embodied in two aspects: On the one hand, the data of the host computer software platform and baseband processing unit are analyzed or packaged, and the data interaction between the two is realized as a relay processing platform; On the other hand, the control message sent by the host computer platform is analyzed and the corresponding control command is generated. The PLC baseband unit can complete the OFDM modulation and demodulation of physical layer data in the low-voltage power line communication mode, and can realize the data interaction with the ARM processing unit. WLC baseband unit can complete OFDM modulation and demodulation of physical layer data in wireless communication mode, and can realize data interaction with ARM processing unit. The PLC digital to analog conversion unit can convert the digital information of the PLC baseband processing unit into analog signals and coupled to the power line. At the same time, the analog signal on the power line can also be collected through the signal coupler, which is converted into a digital signal and transmitted to the PLC baseband processing unit for corresponding processing. WLC digital to analog conversion unit can convert the digital information of WLC baseband processing unit into analog signal, and then use RF module to map the signal to high-frequency subcarrier for transmission. At the same time, the analog signal of the RF module after down-conversion processing can be converted into a digital signal, and then transmitted to the WLC baseband processing unit for corresponding processing.

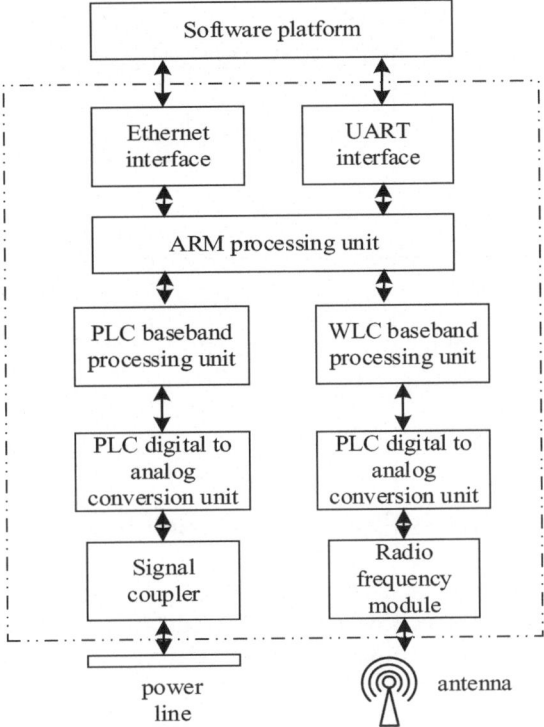

Fig. 1. Dual mode standard transceiver unit overall structure

3 High-Speed Carrier Physical Layer Scheme

In the low voltage power line carrier communication mode, the transmitting end of the physical layer of the high speed power line carrier is coupled to the power line through a series of processing such as coding and modulation. At the receiving end, the signal on the power line is collected and the original data is obtained through a series of processing such as demodulation and decoding, and then transmitted to the data link layer. The structure of the carrier physical layer of the dual-mode standard transceiver unit is shown in Fig. 2.

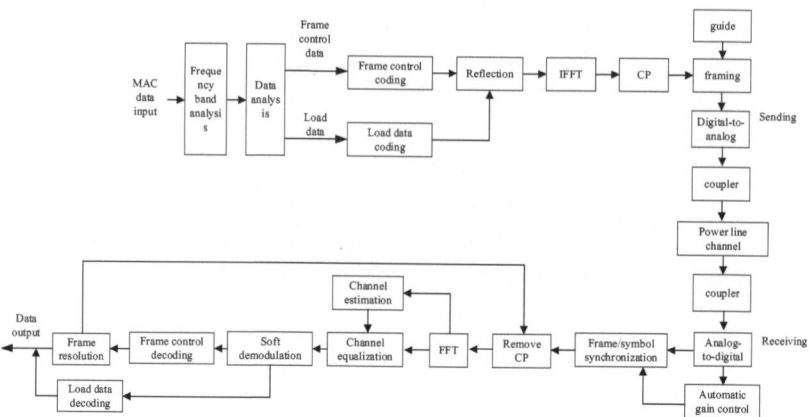

Fig. 2. High-speed carrier hardware overall design structure

4 High-Speed Wireless Physical Layer Solution

In the wireless communication mode, the high-speed wireless physical layer data unit generated after a series of processing such as code modulation is sent to the air through the RF antenna. At the receiving end, the signal in the air is received through the RF antenna,

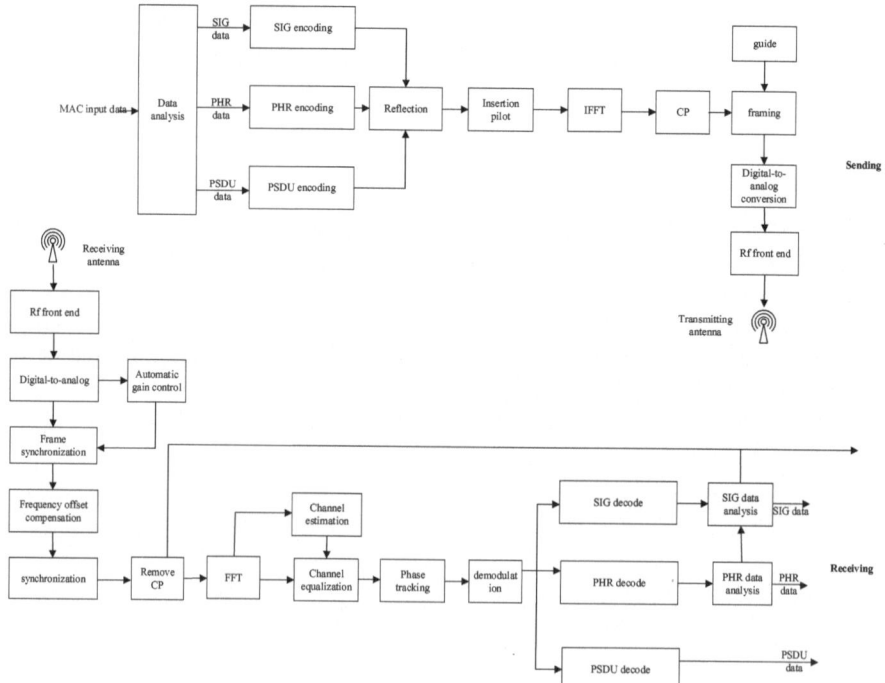

Fig. 3. Schematic diagram of the high-speed wireless physical layer

and then the original data is obtained through a series of processing such as demodulation and decoding, and transmitted to the data link layer for corresponding processing. The structure of the wireless physical layer of the dual-mode standard transceiver unit is shown in Fig. 3.

5 Software Design

Dual-mode standard transceiver unit user space code includes TCP server thread, data link layer processing thread, clock thread. The TCP server thread receives and processes packets at the application layer, the data link layer processing thread processes data at the data link layer received through the power line, and the clock thread maintains the local clock and periodically forwards data set on the software platform to the power line.

A typical C/S structure is formed between the software platform and the dual-mode standard transceiver unit, and the server is built by Select method. In order to improve the speed of application layer message processing, the thread pool method is used to create message processing threads to reduce the time of creating threads. The TCP server thread processing logic is shown in Fig. 4.

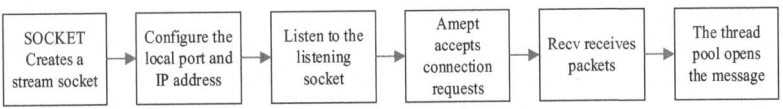

Fig. 4. Access unit TCP server thread

The flowchart of the message processing thread is shown in Fig. 5. In order to realize the function of periodic message forwarding and communication performance test, a custom data structure myusemem is designed to save the information of memory starting point, data length and sending time of data to be sent. The packets received by the application layer are classified into five types: reset packets, time setting packets, performance test packets, scheduled forwarding setting packets, and TEI list setting packets. Each received packet is processed as follows:

1) Reset the message, and the carrier transparent access unit resets the local phase line and clears the sending queue.
2) Time setting message, the carrier transparent access unit corrects the time correction variable and sends the local clock (system time + time correction) to the software platform.
3) The carrier transparent access unit uses the memory pool to store the data to be sent, and uses myusemem to record the information such as the memory starting point, data length, and sending time of the data to be sent, and inserts it into the queue to be sent.
4) Performance test message, the carrier transparent access unit generates the corresponding number of myusemem according to the message and inserts it into the queue to be sent.
5) TEI setting message. The carrier transparent access unit sets the local TEI list according to the message.

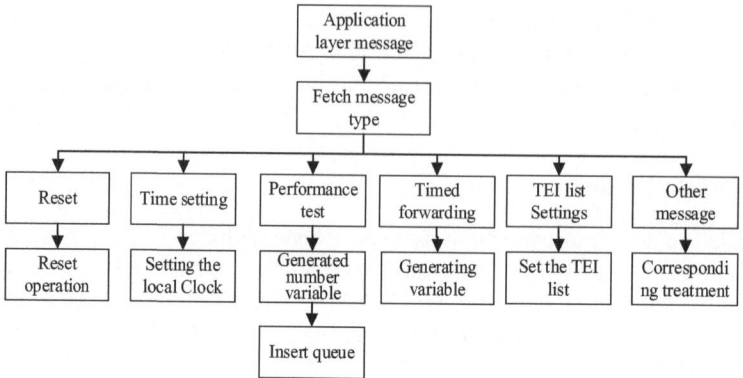

Fig. 5. Access unit message processing thread

6 Simulation Verification

Simulation and verification The software algorithm simulation of the dual-mode standard transceiver unit is implemented using the Matlab simulation tool. The simulation diagrams of key modules of the high-speed power line carrier physical layer and high-speed wireless physical layer are shown below to verify the reliability and realizability of the above system architecture design.

(1) Matlab simulation of high-speed power line carrier physical layer

The Matlab simulation results of frame synchronization, channel estimation, channel equalization and other modules in the HPLC physical layer are shown in Figs. 6, 7, 8 and 9 below.

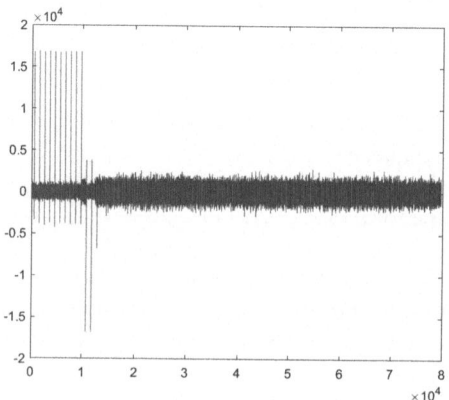

Fig. 6. HPLC synchronous peak

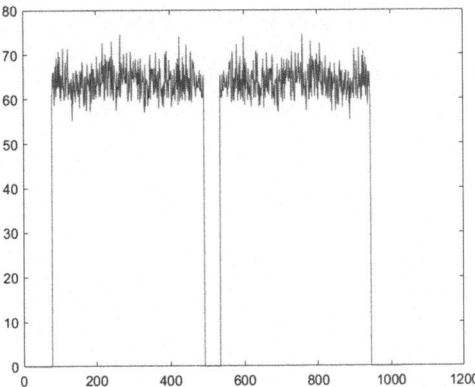

Fig. 7. HPLC channel estimation real part figure

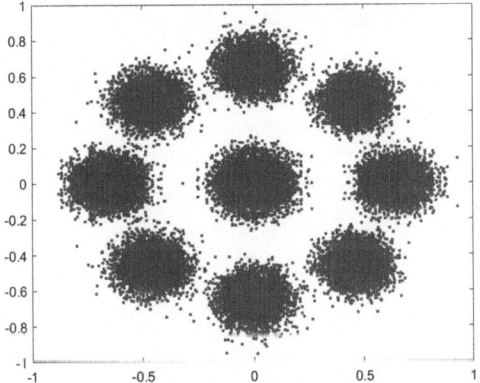

Fig. 8. Constellation before HPLC channel equalization

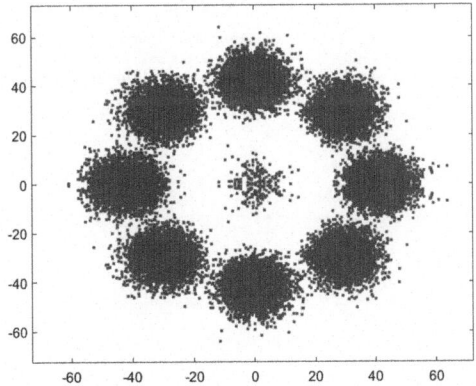

Fig. 9. Constellation after HPLC channel equalization

(2) High-speed wireless physical layer Matlab simulation

The Matlab simulation results of coarse synchronization, fine synchronization and channel equalization modules in the physical layer of HRF are shown in Figs. 10, 11, 12 and 13 below.

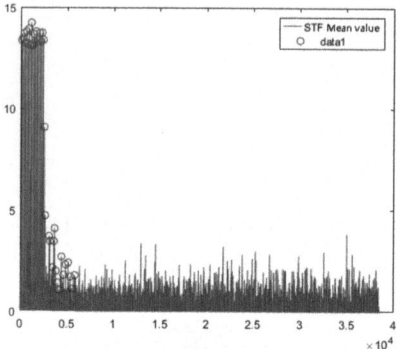

Fig. 10. Peak HRF coarse synchronization

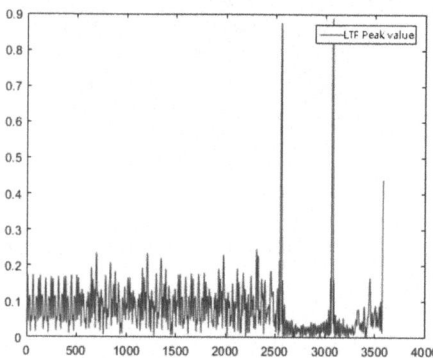

Fig. 11. Peak HRF fine synchronization figure.

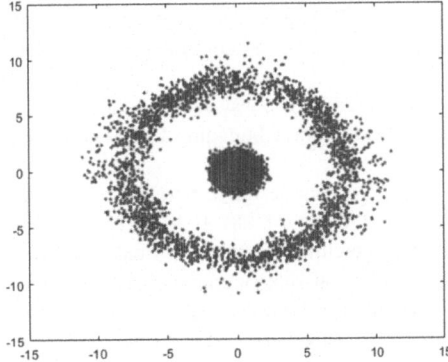

Fig. 12. Constellation diagram before HRF channel balancing

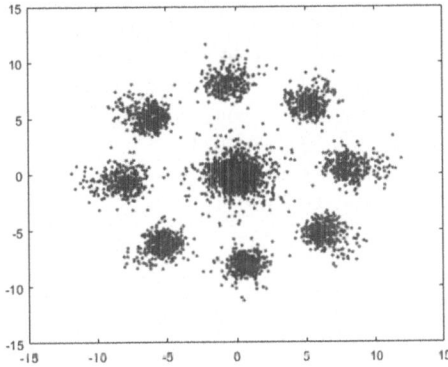

Fig. 13. Constellation diagram after HRF channel balancing

7 Conclusion

In this paper, the interworking technology and detection technology of dual-mode communication are deeply studied, and HPLC and HRF dual-mode standard transceiver unit is designed and implemented, and simulation is carried out. Support Q/GDW 12087.42-2020 《 Dual-mode communication interoperability technical specification Part 42: Data link layer protocol》, Q/GDW 12087.41–2020 《 Dual-mode communication interoperability technical specification part 41: physical layer protocol》 protocol conformance testing, laying a solid foundation for the large-scale application and detection of dual-mode communication units.

References

1. Zhang, C., Ma, X., Xue, L., et al.: Design of monitoring system in low-voltage distribution area based on dual-mode communication technology. Electr. Power Inf. Commun. Technol. **18**(02), 75–79 (2020)

2. Li, B., Luo, Y., Zhang, L., et al.: Simulation test system based on HPLC and micro-power wireless dual-mode communication. Microcontroller Embed. Syst. Appl. **21**(04), 38–40+44 (2021)
3. Ye, J.: Design and implementation of physical layer consistency test system for wideband micro-power communication system. Chongqing University of Posts and Telecommunications (2021)
4. Zhang, C., Wang, D., Zhao, X.: Pilot design of wireless communication in HPLC&RF dual-mode system. Telecommun. Technol. **61**(08), 1020–1025 (2021)
5. Shang, Y.: Research on power line and wireless dual-mode fusion transmission system. Chongqing University of Posts and Telecommunications (2022)
6. Zhang, M.: Key technologies for digital domain suppression of dual channel transceiver mutual coupling interference. University of Electronic Science and Technology of China (2023)
7. Luan, Z., Hua, J., Luo, D., et al.: Design of integrated intelligent measurement platform for HPLC and HRF dual-Mode communication. Mod. Electron. Technol. **46**(22), 159–164 (2019)
8. Ren, Y., Zhang, H., Gao, F., et al.: Design and implementation of forward error correction coding fusion for physical layer of power line carrier and wireless dual-mode communication. Electr. Power Inf. Commun. Technol. **21**(09), 67–74 (2019)
9. Huang, Z., Ren, C.M., Bai, X.Y., et al.: Research and application of micropower wireless communication protocol conformance test for power transmission and transformation equipment. Electrotechnical Eng. (10), 130–133+137 (2024)
10. Chen, G.: Analysis and prospect of heterogeneous dual-mode communication technology. Electron. Technol. **53**(01), 100–103 (2019)

The Mechanisms of Artificial Intelligence Impacting on the Transformation of Family Systems: A Perspective of Complex Adaptive Systems Theory

Jianping Yu[1], Honghua Ma[2], and Yi Li[3(✉)]

[1] School of Marxism, Huazhong University of Science and Technology, Wuhan 430074,, China
[2] School of Optical and Electronic Information, Huazhong University of Science and Technology, Wuhan 430074,, China
[3] School of Marxism, Shenzhen Institute of Information Technology, Shenzhen 518172, China
liyiify@126.com

Abstract. The transformation of family systems is influenced by various complex factors. Compared to economic, cultural, social and other influencing factors, AI(Artificial Intelligence) has a special impact on the transformation of family systems. Based on Complex Adaptive System (CAS) theory, this paper analyzes the mechanisms of AI impacting on the transformation of family systems. CAS theory emphasizes the complexity, adaptability, and nonlinear evolution of phenomena or entities. Within the framework of CAS theory, the transformation of family systems is also regarded as a complex adaptive system, characterized by adaptability and nonlinear dynamics. Through real-time data collection, precise data analysis, and personalized feedback generation, AI enables family systems to develop effective adaptation and feedback mechanisms in response to environmental changes and internal demand adjustments. These adaptation and feedback mechanisms drive the optimization of family decision-making patterns and the restructuring of key elements within the family systems, ultimately influencing transformation of family systems.

Keywords: Artificial Intelligence · The Transformation of Family Systems · Self-Adaptability · Nonlinearity · Complex Adaptive Systems

1 Introduction

As the fundamental unit of social structure, the family systems serve as the cornerstone of societal operation and is also an essential vehicle for cultural transmission. Within the social structure, the family systems play a role in connecting and supporting other elements. The family systems not only provide the initial socialization environment for individual growth and development but also create the conditions for the inter-generational transfer of culture and values. Over time, the family systems have undergone multiple transformations and reconstructions under different social and historical contexts. These changes are typically driven by economic development, social transitions, cultural shifts, and technological advancements. In the 21st century, the rapid development and widespread application of AI are profoundly changing the functioning of various domains, including the family systems. As AI penetrates all aspects of family life, traditional family structures, role distribution, and interaction patterns are facing unprecedented challenges and opportunities. The application scenarios of AI such as smart home, virtual assistants, and online education platforms are reshaping communication methods among family members, decision-making processes, and the power structures within families.

Currently, academic research has extensively explored the application of AI in domestic settings, including its impact on familial emotional relationships [1], roles and responsibilities [2], and mental health [3, 4]. However, despite the deepening application of AI in households, there remains a lack of systematic research on the specific mechanisms of effect on the transformation of family systems. The transformation of family systems refers to systemic changes in the structure, function, form, and value orientations of families. Existing research predominantly focuses on the functionalities and application outcomes of AI itself, while there is a lack of in-depth exploration into how family systems, as complex adaptive systems, respond, adjust, and evolve when faced with the impact of AI. AI, described as "the most important general-purpose technology of our era" [5], influences family systems differently compared to traditional factors, such as economic, cultural, legal and and social factors. The micro-level impacts of AI within domestic settings are primarily reflected in changes in roles and divisions of labor among family members, alterations in family interaction patterns, and shifts in lifestyle. As these micro-level impacts accumulate and become widespread, they have the potential to induce macro-level changes in family structure, function, forms, and ultimately lead to a transformation of the existing family systems.

Therefore, it is necessary to conduct a systematic analysis based on the theory of Complex Adaptive System [6] (CAS) to understand how AI facilitates the transformation of family systems through pathways such as information flow and adaptive feedback mechanisms. Academically, as the fundamental structural unit of society, the transformation of family systems not only reflects the overall development trends of society but also provides a micro-level perspective for understanding broader social changes. By incorporating the theory of CAS, this research aims to reveal the dynamic evolution mechanisms of family systems when confronted with technological shocks, thereby to enrich the theoretical framework of family studies. Additionally, exploring the role of AI in domestic settings can open up new dimensions for the application of CAS theory within the social sciences. From a practical standpoint, as AI becomes increasingly integrated into family life, the trend of transformation of family systems has become a focal point of societal concern. In-depth analysis of the mechanisms through which AI influences family systems can provide with valuable insights for policymakers, family educators, and social service organizations, helping them better address the challenges and opportunities presented by technology. For businesses and technology developers, understanding the profound impact of AI on family systems can facilitate the design and application of more human-centric and family-friendly technologies.

2 The Nonlinear Dynamics of Transformation of Family Systems

Family systems take on different forms across various cultures and societies, yet they are all based on marriage, blood ties, and kinship relationships, involving aspects such as family structures, functions, and forms. As a crucial component of society, family systems not only provide a vital foundation for individual lives but also serve as a key element in social stability and development. As society progresses and transforms, family systems continuously evolve to meet new demands and challenges. Within the analytical framework of CAS theory, the operation of family systems exhibits adaptability, while their transformations demonstrate nonlinear dynamics, reflecting the flexibility and resilience of families in responding to complex environmental changes.

2.1 Self-adaptability

The self-adaptability in the operation of family systems refers to the ability of families to adjust their structures, functions, cultural values, and other aspects in response to external environmental changes, thereby adapting to new circumstances and needs. This self-adaptability enables family systems to flexibly respond to external shocks and internal changes, ensuring their survival and development. In the early 20th century, many sociologists expressed concerns that families might lose their functions and values. William Fielding Ogburn, in his research, pointed out that the basic functions of families such as economic support, reproduction, protection, status granting, education, and religion had already been taken over by other organizations [7]. After World War II, there was a trend among researchers to view the family as a social institution. Many sociologists began to focus on the modernization of the family. Most sociologists believed that families still retained their essential functions and values [8]. The persistence of family functions and values is not unrelated to the self-adaptability of family systems.

Structural Self-adaptation of Family Systems. The structural self-adaptability of family systems is reflected in the dynamic adjustment of family members' composition, role allocation and function allocation. For instance, in response to economic pressures, families may adjust the division of labor between work and education among members, reallocate resources and responsibilities. In some cases, women become the primary breadwinners, while men take on more domestic and childcare responsibilities, indicating a shift from traditional gender roles. In some transnational families, members may live and work in different countries, leveraging the benefits of globalization to share economic responsibilities.

Functional Self-adaptation of Family Systems. The functional self-adaptability of family systems is reflected in the realization of its core functions through functional adjustment and optimization when the family responds to changes in the external environment. Modern families are not merely living spaces; they may integrate multiple functions such as working, studying, entertainment, and health management. For example, in response to technological changes, families might introduce new technologies, e. g., smart homes, online education, to enhance the quality and efficiency of life. Faced with an aging population, families are likely to adapt their care and support to meet the needs of older members.

Cultural and Value Self-adaptation of Family Systems. The self-adaptability of the culture and values of the family systems is reflected in that family members adjust and optimize their culture and values to form a cultural identity and value system with family characteristics when responding to changes in the external environment. For example, in the face of multicultural influences and globalization, families might maintain traditional values while absorbing and integrating new cultural elements. In addition, as societal expectations of family ethics and norms change, families also adjust their internal ethics and norms through self-adaptation mechanisms to better align with societal expectations and standards.

2.2 Abrupt Changes

Family systems can maintain relative stability and continuity over a certain period. However, in constantly changing environmental conditions, transformation of family systems is inevitable. From the perspective of CAS theory, the transformation of family systems is characterized by distinct nonlinear dynamics, that is, changes in family structures, functions, and forms are not linear, gradual or smooth processes. Instead, the transformation of family systems often undergoes a process of gradual accumulation, leading to sudden changes when a certain threshold is reached. As shown in Fig. 1.

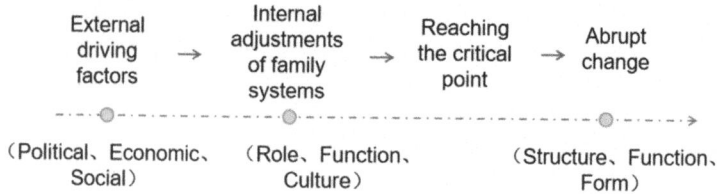

Fig. 1. The Transition from Gradual changes to Abrupt Changes in Family Systems

During periods of stability, family systems adapt to environmental changes through incremental adjustments; whereas during significant transformation periods, abrupt changes become the primary form. This alternation between gradual and abrupt changes imbues the transformation of family systems with both periodicity and complexity.

On the one hand, the transformation of family systems is driven by many factors, which is manifested as gradual change. The interaction of various external factors such as economic development, social and cultural changes, legal and policy adjustments, and technological progress can drive the reform of the family systems. For example, economic factors may alter family income levels, thereby affecting role distribution and functional structures within families. Sociocultural shifts may change family members' values and behavior patterns, influencing interaction modes and organizational forms within families. Additionally, the gradual increase in female employment rates has progressively altered the internal role division within families. When female economic independence becomes widespread, traditional family structures and functions undergo abrupt changes, resulting in the emergence of dual-income families, single-parent families, and other new family forms.

On the other hand, the transformation of family systems often manifests as abrupt changes. These changes sometimes are triggered by major social events or technological advancements. For instance, the Industrial Revolution, post-World War II social reconstruction, and the Information Technology Revolution have all led to rapid changes in family structures and functions. Technological advancements, such as the proliferation of artificial intelligence and the internet, have swiftly altered interaction modes among family members and family management practices. Changes in government policies and laws may also trigger abrupt changes in family systems. For example, policy changes such as family planning policy, reforms in marriage law, and the legalization of same-sex marriage have a direct impact on family size, family composition and marriage relations, resulting in rapid transformations in family systems.

2.3 The Nonlinear by Temporal Factors

The transformation of family systems is not a simple, linear process. Rather, it exhibits dynamic alternation between gradual change and abrupt changes. This characteristic is a typical manifestation of the nonlinearity of family system transformation. The changes of family systems are not achieved overnight. Changes in values, the erosion of traditional influences, and the emergence of new factors all require time, during which time plays a crucial role. The relationship between temporal factors and the nonlinear transformation of family systems is closely intertwined. Over time, small changes within the family systems gradually accumulate. When these accumulations reach a a certain critical point, they can trigger system abrupt changes.

To aid in understanding, we can describe the dynamic changes in the state of family systems S(t) over time t using a nonlinear differential equation. The equation is as follows:

$$dS(t)/dt = \alpha S(t) - \beta S(t)^2$$

where:

α: A positive constant representing the intrinsic driving force or growth rate of transformation of family systems.
β: A positive constant representing the resistance or inhibiting factors in the transformation process.
$dS(t)/dt$: The rate of transformation of family systems state S(t) relative to time t, indicating the speed of transformation of family systems at time t.
$\alpha S(t)$: Represents the linear growth component of the family systems state over time, reflecting the gradual adjustment process of family systems as it adapts to external environmental changes.
$\beta S(t)^2$: Represents the nonlinear growth component of family systems state over time. This reflects the potential for sudden changes or drastic shifts in family systems when a certain threshold is reached.

During the dynamic transformation of family systems, when S(t) is relatively small, the linear growth term $\alpha S(t)$ dominates, and the changes in family systems mainly exhibit gradual adjustments. When S(t) increases to a certain critical point, the nonlinear growth term $\beta S(t)^2$ begins to significantly decrease, and the system may undergo abrupt changes. This illustrates the dynamic alternation between gradual change and transformation of family systems.

3 Special Influence of AI on Family Systems

Technological determinism posits that technological innovation is the primary driving force of social change[9]. The development and application of technology have not only transformed production modes, economic structures, and social relationships but also profoundly influenced the evolution of cultural values and social institutions. Within the transformation of family systems, technological factors have played a key role. Historically, advancements such as the widespread adoption of electricity and the development of communication technologies have significantly impacted on the structure, function, and interaction patterns of families. In the digital age, particularly with the rapid advancement of AI, family systems are once again encountering new pressures for transformation. AI is characterized by efficiency, real-time operation, personalization, and interactivity. Given these distinct features, how does the application of AI within the family settings exert unique influences on the transformation of family systems, compared to other influencing factors such as economic, cultural, and social elements?

3.1 Scientification of Family Decision-Making and Management

The efficiency of AI is based on massive amounts of data, optimizing resources and processes to assist in family decision-making and management, thereby promoting the scientific approach to these activities. First, big data analysis and machine learning algorithms enable AI to quickly process and analyze vast amounts of data within families, providing timely decision support for family members. This immediacy and precision greatly enhance the scientific basis of family management, making decisions more evidence-based. Second, through continuous data collection and analysis, AI systems can adjust and optimize services based on changes in family members' needs, providing flexible and dynamic solutions that make family management more scientific and efficient. Third, AI system through long-term data accumulation and learning, continuously improve service content and methods, and optimize their own service capabilities, so as to achieve scientific family management.

The scientification of family decision-making and management exerts multifaceted impacts on family systems. Firstly, as family decision-making becomes more scientific, traditional roles of family authority may be redefined. Decisions are no longer solely reliant on the experience and judgment of parents or elders, as AI increasingly emerges as a key participant in the decision-making process. This shift is likely to result in adjustments of the internal power structures within families. Moreover, the management and decision-making functions within families are progressively becoming more intelligent. This transition not only has the potential to reduce conflicts and disputes among family members but also enhances the overall operational efficiency of the family, thereby reinforcing its role as an economic and managerial unit. Lastly, with the advancement of AI, the ability to manage families remotely is strengthened, facilitating the development of more cross-regional or virtual family structures. This evolution enables family members to participate in decision-making and management without the need for physical cohabitation.

3.2 Optimization of Family Resource Allocation

The efficiency of AI is reflected in its ability to quickly complete specific tasks with lower time and cost, thereby promoting the sharing and optimal allocation of family resources. First of all, AI can monitor the usage of family resources in real time through data analysis, and provide optimization suggestions through data analysis. This kind of accurate management can reduce the waste of resources and improve the efficiency of resource utilization. Secondly, according to the needs and behavior patterns of family members, AI systems can formulate the optimal resource allocation plan through data analysis to ensure the maximum utilization of family resources and optimize the allocation of resources. Lastly, AI facilitates resource sharing and cooperation among family members. Smart systems through data sharing and collaborative work, optimize the use of family resources and enhance efficiency of family resource utilization.

The optimized allocation of family resources significantly impacts family systems. Firstly, as AI enhances resource distribution, family members may be more inclined to live independently while still maintaining close interaction and resource sharing through AI, making this coexistence of independence and connectivity in family structures to be common. Additionally, AI improves the efficiency of resource management and allocation within families, enabling them to better fulfill their roles in economic support and consumption management. This reduces the burden traditionally placed on a single family member to manage all resource allocation responsibilities and promotes more equitable resource distribution. Furthermore, optimized resources may encourage family members to live in different geographical locations, facilitating more flexible family forms such as transnational or dispersed families through remote resource sharing and services.

3.3 Transformation of Family Daily Life

The real-time capability of AI is reflected in its ability to collect, process, and provide feedback of information in real time, offering customized services to users in areas such as household management, lifestyle preferences, and education and entertainment. First of all, AI realizes the automation and intelligence of household management through smart devices, reduces the housework burden of family members, improves the convenience of life, and changes family daily life. Secondly, AI systems provides personalized and healthy lifestyle services based on habits and preferences of family members by learning their behavior patterns and needs. For example, precision nutrition, smart fitness, chronic disease diagnosis and treatment. Thirdly, the application of AI in family education and entertainment has changed family daily life. By providing personalized educational resources and entertainment content, AI improves the learning efficiency and fun of family members, and changes the way of education and entertainment of families.

The transformation of family daily life has profound implications for family systems. Firstly, as AI becomes more prevalent, routine tasks are taken over by automated systems, gradually altering traditional gender roles and driving the family structure towards greater equality and diversity. Secondly, these transformations of family daily life also enhance the function of the family as a personal support system. Through health monitoring and emotional companionship, AI further strengthens emotional and health-related functions of the family. Finally, the increased convenience in daily life makes geographically dispersed living arrangements more feasible and comfortable for family members, thereby encouraging the formation of new family forms such as virtual or multi-location families.

3.4 Enhanced Emotional Connection and Interaction Among Family Members

AI can engage in bidirectional communication and interaction with users, providing a more natural and human-like interactive experience, thereby strengthening the emotional connections among family members. Firstly, AI enhances emotional connections between family members through affective computing and interactive technology. Intelligent systems can recognize the emotional states of family members and provide appropriate feedback and interaction, improving the quality of emotional communication. Secondly, AI overcomes the limitations of geographical distance on family emotional connections through remote emotional interaction. Intelligent systems enhance emotional connection and interaction among family members by offering high-definition video calls and emotional interaction services. Finally, through applications in emotional support and mental health, AI improves emotional connections and mental health levels of family members. Intelligent systems, through emotional analysis and mental health suggestions, provide appropriate emotional support and mental health services, thereby enhancing the emotional connection and mental well-being of family members.

The changes in emotional connection within families have several significant implications for family systems. Firstly, the enhanced emotional connections facilitated by AI may diminish the sense of physical distance among family members, making complex family structures such as extended or joint families more feasible and stable. Secondly, the emotional support function of the family is further reinforced; as AI not only supports the physical health and well-being of family members but also offers vital emotional support, helping to maintain and strengthen the emotional bonds within the family. Finally, the enhanced emotional interaction enables remote families, such as transnational families or long-distance marriage families, to become more stable, which could become a norm in future family structures due to technological empowerment.

In summary, AI plays a positive role in the transformation of family systems. However, the widespread application of AI within families also presents challenges related to privacy and security. Family members must balance the convenience provided by technology with the need to protect privacy and manage data usage, ensuring that personal information is not misused or poses a threat to family systems. Additionally, family ethics and social equity are also being tested[10]. The applications of AI in families challenge traditional ethical values. Some scholars advocate a conservative stance towards the intervention of artificial intelligence in family life[11]. The introduction of emotional companion robots, for instance, may alter the modes of emotional interaction among family members, potentially causing ethical controversy. Furthermore, the application of AI in families may exacerbate social inequalities. Differences in economic levels among families in accessing and using AI can lead to disparities in education and health management, further widening the social gap.

4 Mechanisms of AI's Impact on Transformation of Family Systems

Within the framework of CAS theory, the operation and transformation of family systems are viewed as complex systems. "In recent years, break throughs in artificial intelligence(AI) and machine learning have revolutionized how we process information, make decisions, and interact with the world."[12] The deep mechanisms through which AI affects transformation of family systems can be systematically analyzed through three levels: "optimization of family decision-making models"as the foundational level, "driving by adaptation and feedback mechanisms"as the intermediate level, and finally reaching "systemic transformation and emergence of new institutions"as the advanced level. These three levels progress sequentially, forming a "bottom-up" logical chain that gradually reveals the mechanisms through which AI impacts transformation of family systems.

4.1 The Promotion of Family Decision-Making Model Optimization Through Data Information Flow

The family decision-making model is a core component of family system operations, involving resource allocation, responsibility sharing, and impacting family members' daily lives, resource distribution, and long-term planning. It reflects the internal power structure and interaction patterns within the family and drives systemic changes in family systems. From CAS theory perspective, data information flow pertains to the transmission and sharing of data information among various components within the system, as well as the decision-making process based on this data information. AI enhances the efficiency of data information flow and information transparency, providing data support and informational basis for family decision-making. This profoundly influences family members' decision-making behaviors and ultimately drives systemic transformation within family systems. As shown in Fig. 2.

Huge amounts of data are the basis for improving decision-making among family members. Through the transmission and sharing of data and information, AI can improve the efficiency and transparency of family information flow. Firstly, AI improves the efficiency of information flow, enabling family members to access information more promptly and accurately. This is manifested in several aspects: through smart devices and sensors, family members can obtain real-time data, such as health status, environmental parameters, and consumption records. AI systems analyze this data to generate useful information. Additionally, AI supports various information delivery channels, including voice assistants, smartphone applications, and wearable devices, ensuring that information is conveyed to family members in the most convenient way. Moreover, smart home systems can instantly share information with all family members, allowing

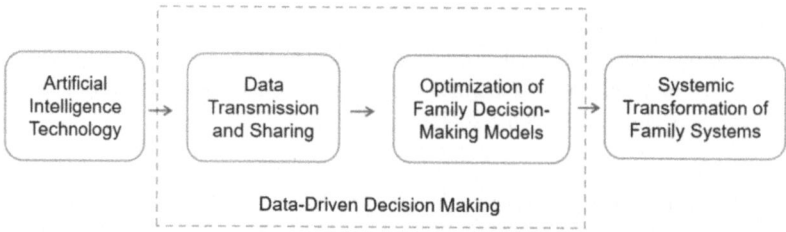

Fig. 2. Diagram of the Process for Optimizing Family Decision-Making Driven by Mass Data Information

them to access the same information, reducing information asymmetry, and increasing information transparency.

The improvement of the efficiency and transparency of family information circulation can promote the optimization of family decision-making models, leading to a transformation in family decision-making patterns. The transformation of family decision-making models has significant implications for family system transformation in the following two aspects: Firstly, it enhances the family's adaptability. In a rapidly changing modern society, families need to continuously adapt to new environments and challenges. AI, by providing data-driven decision support, enables families to respond more quickly and flexibly to external changes. Secondly, it drives the transformation and upgrading of family functions. With the transformation of decision-making models, traditional family functions are redefined and optimized. For example, families are no longer just places for living but have comprehensive platforms for health management, educational guidance, and financial planning. The application of AI makes these functions efficiently realized thereby enhancing the overall functionality and status of the family.

4.2   Adaptation and Feedback Mechanisms Driving the Reconstruction of Key Elements in Family Systems

CAS theory focuses on revealing the constituent elements, motivations and evolution of things or phenomena, with special attention to feedback mechanism and self-adjustment process, which is very important for understanding how family institutions self-adjust and adapt to changes in the external environment. Under the framework of CAS theory, the family system will adjust and adapt to the changes in external environment through feedback mechanism. The powerful data collection, analysis, and processing capabilities of AI form the foundation of these feedback mechanisms. AI enables effective feedback mechanisms in family systems through real-time data collection, precise data analysis, and personalized feedback generation. This allows family systems to adapt to environmental changes and internal demand adjustments. Adaptation and feedback mechanisms drive the optimization of family members' behavior and decision-making, ultimately leading to the self-adjustment and continuous optimization of family systems. Analyzing the key elements of family systems, the self-adjustment and optimization of family systems are mainly reflected in several aspects: the reconstruction of family member roles and responsibilities, the transformation of family lifestyles, the recreation of culture and values, and reconstruction of social network relations. As shown in Fig. 3.

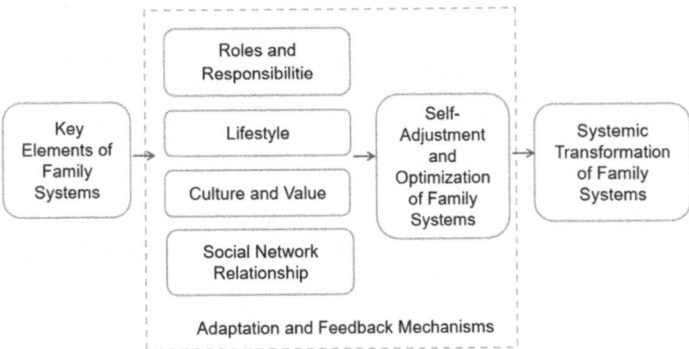

Fig. 3. Diagram of Adaptation and Feedback Mechanism Promoting the Reconstruction of Key Elements of the Household System

Reconstruction of Family Member Roles and Responsibilities. AI systems, through data analysis and real-time feedback, identify behaviors and habits of family members in their daily lives. These feedback mechanisms drive the reallocation and adjustment of roles and responsibilities among family members, resulting in changes to their roles and duties. For example, the use of household robots and smart home devices can alleviate domestic burdens for women, leading to a more equitable division of roles within the family. Smart home systems can monitor family members' activity patterns, suggest and optimize task distribution, improving efficiency and reducing redundant labor. Through these feedback mechanisms, family members can continuously adjust and optimize their roles and responsibilities, achieving more efficient and collaborative family management.

Transformation of Family Lifestyle. AI, with its powerful data collection, analysis, and processing capabilities, drives the transformation of family lifestyles, specifically in behavior patterns and daily activity habits. In terms of behavior patterns, AI can monitor and analyze family members' dietary habits, sleep schedules, and leisure activities, helping them develop healthier lifestyles. For instance, smart health devices can recommend healthy eating plans and appropriate exercise regimens based on family members' health data. Regarding daily habits, smart interventions and optimizations continuously improve lifestyle habits. For example, smart shopping systems analyze family members' purchasing data to recommend suitable products and promotional information, altering previous shopping habits.

Recreation of Culture and Values. AI, through personalized cultural education and value guidance, promotes the dissemination and consensus of values among family members. For example, smart education platforms can regularly provide suggestions for family cultural activities, such as joint reading and cultural festivals, helping family members consolidate and internalize new cultures and values in practice. Cultural feedback mechanisms can foster a shared cultural identity and value system among family members during the adaptation process, enhancing family cohesion and cultural heritage.

Reconfiguration of Social Network Relationships. Social network relationships include interactions among family members, friendships, coworker collaborations, and community support. AI, with its powerful data collection, analysis, and processing capabilities, can monitor and analyze social network relationships in real time through social media, smart home devices, and other information technology tools. The application of this technology changes traditional modes of social interaction, making human interactions less confined by geographical space and more dependent on virtual spaces and digital platforms. The reconfiguration of social network relationships is primarily achieved through changes in information flow and interaction frequency, the rise of social platforms and virtual communities, and intelligent recommendations and personalized services.

4.3 Systemic Transformation of Family Systems and Emergence of New Institutions

The operation of modern family systems largely depends on the allocation and management of time and space. Key components of family functioning include members' schedules, work hours, educational time, living environment, activity spaces, and resource distribution. AI promotes interaction and adjustment among various family subsystems by reorganizing time and space. Over time, through ongoing interaction, adjustment, and accumulation, this process can trigger deep internal restructuring of the system, systematically altering the structure and functions of the family systems. As AI becomes more widespread and deeply integrated, the family systems continuously undergoes self-adjustment and optimization, leading to the emergence of new family system models. As shown in Fig. 4.

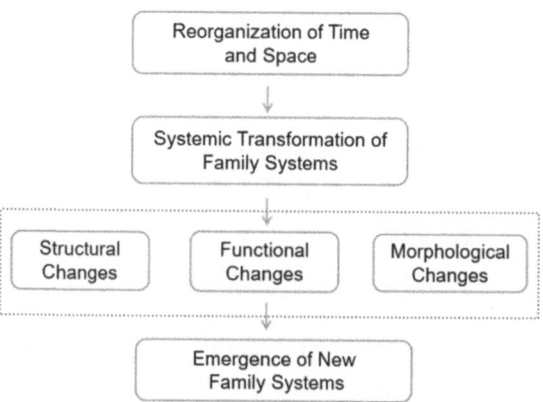

Fig. 4. Transformation happens and Emergence of New Family Systems

First of all, it is necessary to clarify the reorganization of time and space and its systemic impact. AI breaks the traditional constraints of time and space within family settings, optimizing and rearranging time management and space utilization to drive systemic transformation of family systems. On one hand, traditional family time management is often constrained by fixed work hours and regular family life rhythms, which can hinder interaction and collaboration among family members. With the application of AI in family contexts, intelligent scheduling and automated management can optimize family members' time arrangements. The optimization of family time is analogous to the relativity of time in special relativity theory; each family member's time schedule is no longer absolute but relative and personalized. On the other hand, traditional family space utilization is limited by physical constraints, with family members' activity ranges typically confined to fixed living spaces. Smart home systems and devices can optimize the use and management of family spaces. The optimization and reorganization of space are similar to the curvature and influence of matter and energy on spacetime in general relativity; AI achieves optimized use of physical space through intelligent management.

The dynamics of system evolution essentially originate from within the system, where interactions among micro-level entities generate macro-level complex phenomena. The application of AI in family settings optimizes family decision-making models and reconstructs key elements of family systems. Through the reorganization of time and space, AI ultimately drives systemic transformation in family system. The outcomes include more diverse and flexible family structures, more intelligent and varied family functions, and increasingly complex and diverse family forms, leading to the emergence of new family system.

In terms of family structure, besides traditional nuclear families, extended families, and single-parent families, new forms of families have emerged. For example, inter-generational families and cooperative families, showing a trend of diversification. At the same time, the roles and responsibilities of family members within the family have become more flexible, adapting to different family needs and lifestyles. Regarding to family functions, smart technologies endow families with enhanced management and operational capabilities. It not only improves the efficiency of traditional functions such as household management, health monitoring, and educational guidance but also fosters new functional areas, such as smart home management and personalized services, greatly enriching the content and forms of family life. In terms of family forms, the integration of different family forms and functions results in diverse and complex characteristics, with profound changes in interaction patterns among family members, internal management methods, and connections with external society.

In the process of the systemic change of family systems, some new phenomena, characteristics or patterns have emerged. It includes the emergence of new family models, the formation of innovative ways of interaction, and the continuous evolution of family roles and responsibilities. The new family models primarily include smart families and virtual families. Some scholars currently express cautious concern regarding to the involvement of virtual family members in family life, and this issue will not be explored in depth here. However, it is undeniable that the emergence of virtual family members has the potential to trigger a reconstruction of the family ecosystem [13]. On one hand, with the continuous advancement of AI, the role of virtual family members such as smart robots and virtual assistants within the family will increase. The interaction among virtual family members and human family members will become more frequent and close, leading to an ongoing evolution of human family members' roles and responsibilities. On the other hand, interactions among human family members and smart devices have become a regular part of family system models. Smart home assistants, through efficient task execution and real-time feedback mechanisms, will take on more daily tasks and management responsibilities, allowing human family members to focus on higher-level activities and goals. In summary, the applications of AI have driven systemic transformation in family systems, leading to the emergence of new family systems.

5 Conclusion

Based on CAS theory, this paper analyzes the mechanism of how AI influences the transformation of family systems from three aspects: the optimization of decision-making models facilitated by data and information flow, the restructuring of key elements in family system driven by adaptation and feedback mechanisms, and the systemic transformation and emergence of new family systems. The study reveals that applications of AI in family settings optimize decision-making processes and reconstructs critical elements of family systems. Through the reorganization of time and space, these changes ultimately drive systemic transformations in the family structure, which are characterized by the dynamic alternation between gradual and abrupt changes and reflects the complex adaptability of family systems when facing external technological impacts.

Firstly, applications of AI enhances the internal information flow and decision-making efficiency within families, thereby optimizing the decision-making models. This optimization is evidenced by family members' ability to obtain and respond to information more quickly and accurately in daily decision-making, thus improving the overall operational efficiency of family systems. Secondly, the adaptation and feedback mechanisms are further strengthened under the influence of AI, enabling the family systems to respond more promptly to environmental changes and internal needs, thereby achieving self-adjustment and continuous optimization. Finally, over time, these gradual changes induced by AI accumulate and ultimately drive systemic transformations in the family structure, leading to the emergence of new family system forms.

Although this study has made certain progress in uncovering the mechanisms by which AI impacts transformation of family systems, there are some limitations. Firstly, the research is primarily framed within CAS theory. While this theory provides a robust tool for understanding the complexity of family systems, its application has certain limitations. In particular, CAS theory may overlook some critical intermediary mechanisms when addressing complex relationships among individual behaviors at the micro-level and societal institutional changes at the macro-level. Secondly, the study mainly focuses on the role of AI within family systems and does not fully account for the combined effects of other technological or socio-economic factors, which could lead to a somewhat one-sided explanation of transformation of family systems. Additionally, different cultural and regional contexts also present significant limitations. The structure, function, and transformation pathways of family systems may vary considerably across different cultural and regional backgrounds.

Therefore, future research could delve deeper into the influence of AI on transformation of family systems in diverse cultural contexts, analyzing the universality and particularity of these impacts across different cultural and regional landscapes. Such cross-cultural and cross-regional comparative studies could provide more comprehensive theoretical support and practical guidance for understanding transformation of family systems on a global scale.

Acknowledgements. This research was supported by Research on the Innovation of Teaching Paradigm and Practical Exploration of Ideological and Political Theory Courses in Institutes Based on Large Language Model (No. 2023GXSZ169) and Research on the Improvement Strategy of Teaching Effects of Ideological and Political Theory Courses in Institutes Based on Large Language Model (No. Szjy23012).

References

1. Thomas, P.A. , Liu, H. , Umberson, D. : Family Relationships and Well-Being. Innovation in Aging 1(3), igx025 (2017)
2. Hertlein, K.M.: Digital dwelling: technology in couple and family relationships. Fam. Relat. **61**(3), 374–387 (2012)
3. Guo, Y.: Examining the impact of assistive technology on psychological health, family education, and curriculum research in Japan: Insights from Artificial Intelligence. J. Autism Dev. Disord. (2023). https://doi.org/10.1007/s10803-023-06105-4
4. Zhao, J., Wu, M., Yun, L., Wang, X., Jia, J.: Cognitive psychology-based artificial intelligence review. Frontiers in Neuroscience (2022). https://doi.org/10.3389/fnins.2022.1024316
5. Brynjolfsson, E. , McAfee, A.: Artificial intelligence, for real. Harvard Business Review (2017). https://starlab-alliance.com/wp-content/uploads/2017/09/AI-Article.pdf
6. Holland, J.H.: Studying complex adaptive systems. J. Syst. Sci. Complexity **19**(1), 1–8 (2006)
7. Ogburn, W.F.: Social Change with Respect to Culture and Original Nature, pp. 237–256. B. W. HUEBSCH Press, New York (1922)
8. Bengtson, V.L.: Beyond the nuclear family: the increasing importance of multigenerational bonds. J. Marriage Fam. **63**(1), 1–16 (2001)
9. Paragas, F. de la C., Lin, T.T.C.: Organizing and reframing technological determinism. New Media Soc. **18**(8), 1528–1546 (2014)
10. Calo, R.: Robots and privacy. In: Lin, P., Abney, K., Bekey, G.A. (eds.) Robot Ethics: The Ethical and Social Implications of Robotics, pp. 187–201. MIT Press, Cambridge (2012)
11. Hu, S.: The ethical limits and philosophical reflections on family support provided by Artificial Intelligence. J. Northeastern Univ. (Soc. Sci. Ed.) **26**(03), 145–152 (2024)
12. Ahmed, B.: The dynamics of family structures in modern society: shifting patterns and evolving definitions. Liberal J. Lang. Literat. Rev. **2**(1), 57–68 (2024)
13. Zhang, S., Ma, B.: Home redefined: concerns about the impact of humanoid intelligence on human family relationships. Media Watch **16**(06), 201–209 (2021)

A Blockchain PoW Consensus Mechanism Based on Edge Computing in the IoVs

Liya Xu[1], Mingzhu Ge[2]([✉]) [ID], Caicai Zhang[3], Jiaoli Shi[1], Xiwei Dong[1], and Hongbo Li[4]

[1] Jiujiang University, Jiujiang 332005, Jiangxi, China
[2] Taizhou Vocational College of Science and Technology, Taizhou 318020, Zhejiang, China
mingzhug@whu.edu.cn
[3] Zhejiang Polytechnic University of Mechanical and Electrical Engineering, Hangzhou 310000, Zhejiang, China
[4] Daqing Normal University, Daqing 163712, Heilongjiang, China

Abstract. The explosive increase of vehicles and the emergence of novel businesses such as driverless driving have presented fresh challenges to the data security of the IoVs (Internet of Vehicles). To ensure data security, a trusted decentralized distributed storage approach for managing and storing information proves to be a feasible solution. The blockchain enables distributed nodes to jointly maintain a consistent and tamper-proof ledger, facilitating trusted storage and transmission of information among distributed nodes. However, the consensus mechanism of the blockchain demands that miners in the system possess strong computing power for mining computations. Unfortunately, the performance of nodes in the IoVs is limited and fails to meet these requirements, significantly restricting the application of the blockchain in the IoVs. This paper proposes a blockchain consensus mechanism based on edge computing, with roadside node RSU serving as the edge server to undertake the task of miners for mining, in order to address the issues of insufficient computing power and unstable topology of vehicle nodes. Simulation experiments indicate that the consensus mechanism proposed in this paper has lower total costs, including total energy consumption and delay, compared to the PoW consensus mechanism that uses vehicle nodes as miners.

Keywords: Edge Computing · IoVs · Blockchain · Consensus Mechanism · PoW

1 Introduction

The research and development of intelligent vehicles and driverless technologies have transformed automobiles from mere transportation means into service platforms integrating office and entertainment functions [1]. The trusted storage and sharing of data among vehicles is of vital importance for enhancing driving safety, especially in the future driverless environment [2]. When malicious nodes exist in the IoVs, they may release false information or tamper with the true information transmitted by other vehicle nodes, causing receivers to make erroneous decisions, which may lead to traffic accidents and severe consequences.

J. Zeng and L.-J. Zhang (Eds.): EDGE 2024, LNCS 15424, pp. 74–81, 2025.
https://doi.org/10.1007/978-3-031-77069-2_6

To guarantee data security, a trusted decentralized distributed storage approach is requisite in the IoVs for managing and storing information. The blockchain enables distributed nodes to jointly maintain a consistent and tamper-proof ledger, facilitating trusted storage and transmission of information among distributed nodes, and it exhibits a high degree of security and reliability [3]. Blockchain technology includes data encryption [4–6], consensus mechanisms, smart contracts and P2P transmission, which can be used in cloud computing [7, 8] and edge computing environments. Blockchain technology can assist unfamiliar nodes in establishing trusted transmission in an untrusted environment [9]. It can not only record financial transactions in digital currency applications, but also play a significant role in non-financial fields such as industry and transportation [10].

One of the key technologies for implementing the blockchain is the consensus mechanism. Nodes reach consensus based on this mechanism and jointly maintain a consistent ledger. The process of reaching a consensus is a competitive computing process known as "mining". The participating nodes are referred to as "miners". Miners compete to calculate the HASH problem. The first miner to calculate the result and have it verified acquires the right to keep the accounts and adds their packaged block to the blockchain. This demands that miners in the blockchain network must possess strong computing power to win this competition. However, the on-board equipment performance of vehicle nodes in the IoVs is limited, and the network topology is extremely unstable, failing to meet the requirements of the above-mentioned competitive "mining" for reaching consensus. Applying the blockchain to the IoVs presents the following challenges:

(1) Vehicle nodes are not competent for the role of miners. In the IoVs, the computing power of a single vehicle node is limited and does not meet the requirements.
(2) The classic consensus mechanism and P2P propagation mechanism in the blockchain are only applicable to network environments with stable topologies. In the IoVs, vehicle nodes move at high speeds, and the topology is extremely unstable, which does not conform to the traditional application environment and cannot be applied.

To address the aforementioned issues, this paper employs roadside node RSU as an edge server to undertake the task of blockchain miners and proposes a blockchain consensus mechanism based on edge computing. Compared with vehicle nodes, RSU features a more stable network topology, more reliable communication channels, and stronger computing and storage capabilities. These advantages render RSU a feasible choice as a miner for the blockchain in the IoVs environment.

2 Internet of Vehicles System Model

2.1 Network Model

As illustrated in Fig. 1, the network model herein is constituted by vehicle nodes and roadside units (RSU). Among these, each RSU not only holds its available computing resources but also serves as a relay node to facilitate information interaction among vehicle nodes within its communication coverage. $R = \{R_1, R_{2,...,}R_h\}$ constitutes the set of RSUs.

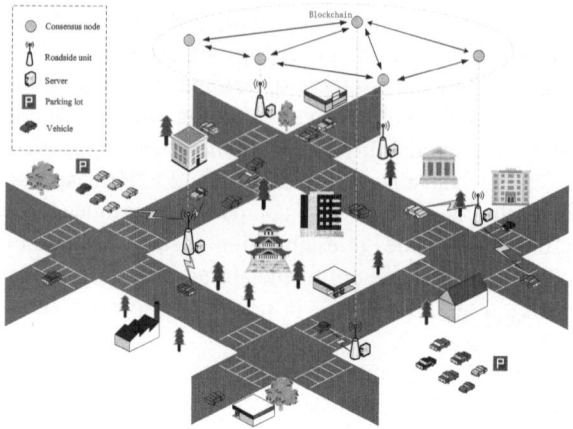

Fig. 1. Network Model

In the blockchain system, the blockchain nodes comprise all RSUs, which are responsible for generating new blocks and conducting the consensus process. The blockchain system guarantees data transmission and sharing among RSUs on the precondition that the computed result data is not maliciously tampered with, enabling RSUs to share data securely and reliably. Accordingly, when a vehicle node generates a computationally intensive task during driving, it opts to transfer the task to the RSU. After the RSU accomplishes the computation, it is stored on the blockchain to realize data sharing among RSUs. Even if the vehicle moves out of the current RSU coverage, it can obtain the task result through the blockchain system without the computed result data being maliciously tampered with.

2.2 Task Model

The computing task is defined as $I_{MV}(t) \triangleq \{B_{MV}(t), C_{MV}(t)\}$, where $B_{MV}(t)$ represents the size of the input data required for the task $I_{MV}(t)$, and $C_{MV}(t)$ denotes the total number of CPU cycles necessary to complete the task IMV(t), that is, the computing resources needed for task completion.

Define $OD(t) \in \{0, 1, 2, ..., n, ..., N\}$ as the upload decision of the computing task. When $OD(t) = 0$, it implies that the task will be uploaded to the RSU for computation. $OD(t) = 1$ indicates that the task is uploaded to R_1 for execution, and when $OD(t) = n$, it means the decision to upload the task to R_n for execution.

2.3 Communication Model

The vehicle node uploads the task $I_{MV}(t)$ to the RSU. According to Shannon's Second Theorem, the rate [11] $R_{V2I}(t)$ when MV transmits data to the RSU is defined as Eq. (1).

$$R_{V2I}(t) = W \log_2 (1 + \frac{P_{V2I}(t)g_0 \psi d_{V2I}(t)^{-\varepsilon}}{I + \Xi^2})$$ (1)

In the equation, W represents the channel bandwidth between the vehicle and the RSU, $P_{V2I}(t)$ indicates the transmission power of the vehicle node, g_0 represents the path loss constant, ψ and $d_{V2I}(t)$ represent the fading channel power gain and the distance from the vehicle node to the RSU covering the vehicle respectively, I is the maximum received interference power, ε is the path loss exponent, and Ξ^2 is Gaussian noise. Therefore, the transmission delay $T_{tr,R}(t)$ when the task $I_{MV}(t)$ is offloaded to the RSU is Eq. (2),

$$T_{tr,R}(t) = \frac{B_{MV}(t)}{R_{V2I}(t)} \tag{2}$$

and the corresponding transmission energy consumption $E_{tr,R}(t)$ is Eq. (3).

$$E_{tr,R}(t) = P_{V2I}(t) \cdot \frac{B_{MV}(t)}{R_{V2I}(t)} \tag{3}$$

The RSU uploads the result to the blockchain system, and through consensus, secure and tamper-proof sharing among RSUs is accomplished. The delay of the blockchain system is defined as $T_{bc}(t)$, and the energy consumption is defined as $E_{bc}(t)$. This process will be elaborated in detail in the blockchain section.

Therefore, in this case, the communication delay is Eq. (4),

$$T_{tr,Rall}(t) = T_{tr,R}(t) + T_{bc}(t) \tag{4}$$

and the total communication energy consumption is calculated as Eq. (5).

$$E_{tr,Rall}(t) = E_{tr,R}(t) + E_{bc}(t) \tag{5}$$

2.4 Computational Model

Assume that the current MV moves within the communication coverage of the h-th RSU, and F_{R_h} is represented as the computing capacity of the h-th RSU (that is, the number of CPU cycles per second). Consequently, the processing delay and energy consumption of the task $I_{MV}(t)$ are computed as Eq. (6) and Eq. (7), respectively.

$$T_{comp,R}(t) = \frac{C_{MV}(t)}{F_{R_h}(t)} \tag{6}$$

$$E_{comp,R}(t) = P_{R_h}(t) \cdot \frac{C_{MV}(t)}{F_{R_h}(t)} \tag{7}$$

In the equations, $P_{R_h}(t)$ is the power consumption of the h-th RSU for processing the task.

To sum up, when the RSU acts as the miner to carry out the mining task, the total system delay and total energy consumption are Eq. (8) and Eq. (9), respectively.

$$T(t) = T_{tr,R}(t) + T_{bc}(t) + T_{comp,R}(t) \tag{8}$$

$$E(t) = E_{tr,R}(t) + E_{bc}(t) + E_{comp,R}(t) \tag{9}$$

3   Block Generation

RSU (miner) packs transactions in chronological order into new blocks and subsequently computes the HASH puzzle. Once the result is obtained, it appends its signature and broadcasts it to other nodes for verification. When the verification is passed by more than 51% of the total number of nodes (N), consensus is achieved, and the block is broadcasted. The block generation process primarily consists of two steps: miners packaging transactions and all miner nodes reaching consensus based on the PoW consensus mechanism.

(1) Transaction packaging. Assume the number of consensus nodes is K (K ≥ N). At this stage, it is necessary to calculate the HASH puzzle, generate a signature, and K-1 authentication codes AC. Suppose the miner R_i requires θ CPU cycles to calculate the HASH puzzle, α CPU cycles to generate the signature, and β CPU cycles to generate the authentication code. The required CPU cycle for this time is $\Delta_{R_i} = \theta + \alpha + \beta$. Then, the calculation delay and energy consumption of the miner are represented as Eq. (10) and Eq. (11), respectively.

$$T_{R_i}^{comp} = \frac{\Delta_{R_i}}{F_{R_i}} \tag{10}$$

$$E_{R_i}^{comp} = P_{R_i}(t) \cdot \frac{\Delta_{R_i}}{F_{R_i}(t)} \tag{11}$$

$F_{R_i}(t)$ is the computing capability of R_i and $P_{R_i}(t)$ is the computing power of R_i.

(2) Reaching consensus. When the consensus node receives no fewer than K submission messages and they are verified and passed, the consensus is attained this time. The new block is officially generated and broadcast to all nodes, and the ledgers of all nodes are synchronously updated. The consensus node needs to verify K signatures and AC. Thus, the CPU cycles required by the consensus node is $\Delta_{con,R_i} = K(\alpha + \beta)$. Therefore, the calculation delay and energy consumption at this stage are calculated as Eq. (12) and Eq. (13), respectively.

$$T_{con}^{comp}(t) = \max_{R_K \in R'} \{ \frac{\Delta_{con,R_K}}{F_{R_K}(t)} \} \tag{12}$$

$$E_{con}^{comp}(t) = \sum_{i=1}^{K} P_{R_i}(t) \cdot \frac{\Delta_{con,R_K}}{F_{R_i}(t)} \tag{13}$$

In summary, the delay $T_{cons}(t)$ and energy consumption $E_{cons}(t)$ generated during the consensus process are respectively represented as $T^{comp}(t) = T_{R_i}^{comp}(t) + T_{con}^{comp}(t)$ and $E^{comp}(t) = E_{R_i}^{comp}(t) + E_{con}^{comp}(t)$.

4   Performance Analysis

To accelerate the convergence and effectiveness of the proposed optimization scheme, in this paper, the network model is simplified during the simulation process and only a small-scale research environment is considered. Hence, the following parameter settings are made in Table 1.

Table 1. Simulation parameters

Parameters	Values
Number of blockchain nodes (number of RSU) N	6
Number of blockchain consensus nodes K	4
Number of CPU cycles required to generate/verify a MAC θ	2M cycles
Number of CPU cycles required to generate/verify a signature ϕ	1M cycles
Average transaction size L	200 B
Average computing power of RSU FR	3 GHz
Transmission power of RSU PR	1000 mW
Transmission power of MV PP	100 mW
Weight of delay in total cost $\sigma 1$	0.3
Weight of energy consumption in total cost $\sigma 2$	0.7

Figure 2 depicts the variations in the total system energy consumption under different task complexities. It can be observed from the figure that as the task complexity increases, the total system energy consumption rises significantly. The curve of the vehicles as miners scheme exhibits the fastest upward trend. The reason is that when the vehicles acted as the miners strategy confronts more complex computing tasks, the processing efficiency is low, which considerably increases the computing energy consumption.

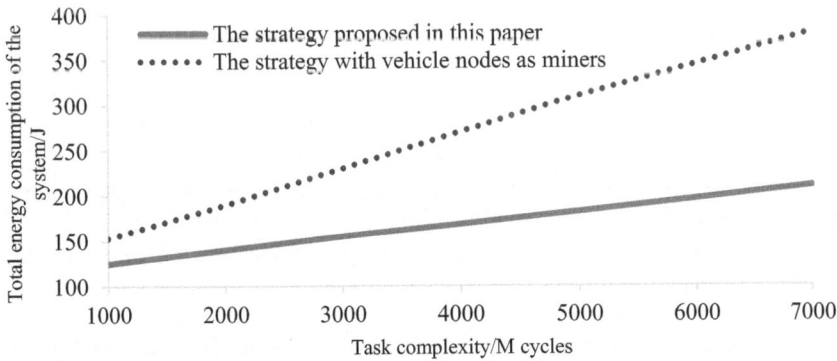

Fig. 2. Total energy consumption of the system vs task complexity

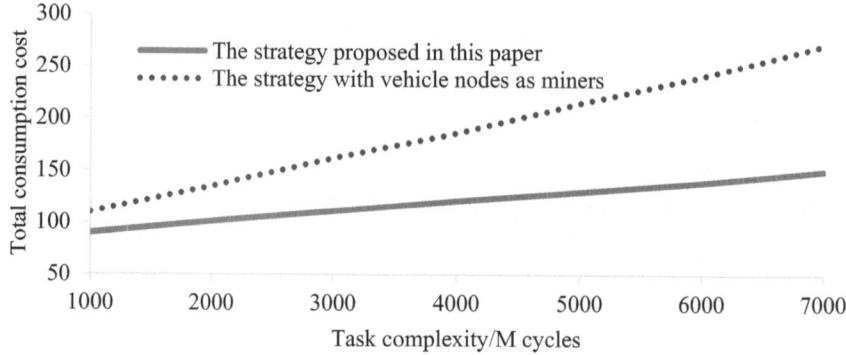

Fig. 3. Total consumption cost vs task complexity

Figure 3 shows the relationship curves between the total system cost and the task complexity produced by two different schemes when handling the same task, with the task data volume being a fixed value of 200 kB. It can be observed that the total system cost of all schemes increases as the task complexity grows. Among them, the total cost generated based on the proposed in this paper is relatively lower than other scheme. The reason is that when the task complexity increases, the system inevitably consumes more time and energy. However, reasonable offloading decisions, appropriate block sizes, and magnitudes can reduce latency and optimize energy consumption.

5 Summary

In light of the issues that the on-board equipment performance of vehicle nodes in the IoVs is limited, the network topology is extremely unstable, and vehicle nodes cannot undertake the miner tasks in the blockchain, this paper proposes that roadside node RSU be utilized as the miner in the IoVs blockchain to execute the mining tasks. Compared with vehicle nodes, roadside node RSU possesses a more stable network topology, a more reliable communication channel, and stronger computing and storage capabilities. Simulation experiments indicate that the consensus mechanism proposed in this paper has lower total costs, such as total energy consumption and delay, compared with the strategy with vehicles as miners.

Acknowledgment. This work is supported by the National Science Foundation of China (No. 62341206, 62062045), Jiangxi Natural Science Foundation (No. 20232BAB202053), Zhejiang Province Visiting Engineer Cooperation Project (No. FG2023061), Natural Science Fund of Heilongjiang Province in 2022 (No. LH2022G001).

References

1. Fang, Y., Min, H., Wu, X., Wang, W., Zhao, X., Mao, G.: On-ramp merging strategies of connected and automated vehicles considering communication delay. IEEE Trans. Intell. Transp. Syst. **23**(9), 15298–15312 (2022)

2. Zhang, J., Li, T., Mohammad, S.O., Lin, C., Ma, J.: Enabling efficient data sharing with auditable user revocation for IoV systems. IEEE Syst. J. **16**(1), 1–12 (2021)
3. Li, X., Zheng, Z., Dai, H.: When services computing meets blockchain: challenges and opportunities. J. Parallel Distrib. Comput. **150**, 1–14 (2021)
4. Mei, Z., et al.: Secure multi-dimensional data retrieval with access control and range query in the cloud. Inf. Syst. **122**, 102343 (2024)
5. Yao, S., Ralph, V.J.D., In-Ho, R., Xu, L., Mei, Z., Shi, J.: An identity-based proxy re-encryption scheme with single-hop conditional delegation and multi-hop ciphertext evolution for secure cloud data sharing. IEEE Trans. Inf. Forensics Secur. **18**, 3833–3848 (2023)
6. Wu, Z., Liu, H., Xie, J., Xu, D., Li, G., Lu, C.: An effective method for the protection of user health topic privacy for health information services. World Wide Web **26**, 3837–3859 (2023)
7. Feng, J., Yang, L.T., Zhang, R., Qiang, W., Chen, J.: Privacy preserving high-order bi-lanczos in cloud-fog computing for industrial applications. IEEE Trans. Ind. Inform **18**, 7009–7018 (2020)
8. Feng, J., Yang, L.T., Zhu, Q., Choo, K.K.R.: Privacy-preserving tensor decomposition over encrypted data in a federated cloud environment. IEEE Trans. Dependable Secur. Comput **17**, 857–868 (2018)
9. Pratima, S., Suyel, N., Ruben, G., Javier, P., Munesh, C.: EHDHE: enhancing security of healthcare documents in IoT-enabled digital healthcare ecosystems using blockchain. Inf. Sci. **629**, 703–718 (2023)
10. Fan, L., et al.: A secured vehicle brain: DAO-based collaborative perception and decision-making systems for intelligent vehicles in CPSS. IEEE Trans. Intell. Veh. **9**(1), 52–54 (2024)
11. Ma, C., Zhu, J., Liu, M., Zhao, H., Liu, N., Zou, X.: Parking edge computing: parked-vehicle-assisted task offloading for urban VANETs. IEEE Internet Things J. **8**(11), 9344–9358 (2021)

Analysis of the Operational Characteristics and Impact of Large-Scale Integration of Supercharging Equipment in Shenzhen

Yiguan Ma[1] and Xing Wang[2]([✉])

[1] Shenzhen Polytechnic University, Shenzhen 518055, Guangdong, People's Republic of China
[2] Shenzhen Urban Planning & Land Resources Research Center, Shenzhen 518034, People's Republic of China
479794507@qq.com

Abstract. The rapid growth of new energy vehicles (NEVs) in Shenzhen has necessitated the expansion of the city's supercharging infrastructure. As of June 2023, Shenzhen has established a comprehensive charging network with over 7,600 stations and 190,000 facilities, including 44 supercharging stations. This study analyzes the operational characteristics and impacts of these supercharging stations on the local distribution network. Through clustering analysis of charging load data from 20 typical stations, four distinct load patterns were identified: "Multiple Peaks in a Day," "Noon Peak," "Morning Valley and Evening Peak," and "Flat." The study highlights the influence of user travel habits and charging costs on these patterns. Additionally, variations in load characteristics between weekdays and weekends were observed, indicating changes in user behavior. The findings provide insights into the efficient integration of supercharging facilities into urban power grids and support the strategic planning of future infrastructure development in line with Shenzhen's "Supercharging City" initiative.

Keywords: Supercharging stations · new energy vehicles · charging load features · operational efficiency

1 Introduction

The theoretical framework surrounding EV charging and power grid interaction primarily focuses on load management and optimization strategies. Zhang and Wang (2020) emphasize the importance of understanding the dynamic nature of EV charging demand and its implications for grid stability. They propose models that predict load variations based on charging patterns, highlighting the need for adaptive grid management systems.Li and Chen (2019) explore the spatial distribution of charging stations and its theoretical impact on urban power grids. Their work underscores the necessity of strategically locating charging stations to minimize grid congestion and enhance load distribution. The authors advocate for the integration of smart grid technologies to facilitate real-time load balancing and demand response.

J. Zeng and L.-J. Zhang (Eds.): EDGE 2024, LNCS 15424, pp. 82–94, 2025.
https://doi.org/10.1007/978-3-031-77069-2_7

Wang and Liu (2021) provide a comprehensive review of optimization models for charging infrastructure, focusing on minimizing the adverse effects of peak load demand. They argue that incorporating renewable energy sources into the charging network can mitigate the impact on the grid, aligning with sustainable energy goals. Empirical research has provided valuable insights into the real-world implications of EV charging on power grids. Zhao and Sun (2020) conducted a case study on fast charging stations in urban areas, revealing significant fluctuations in grid load during peak charging hours. Their findings suggest that fast charging stations, while convenient, pose challenges to grid stability due to their high power demand. Liu and Gao (2019) empirically assess the impact of EV charging on grid stability through simulation models. Their study demonstrates that unmanaged charging can lead to voltage instability and increased operational costs. They propose demand-side management strategies, such as time-of-use pricing, to incentivize off-peak charging and alleviate grid stress.

Xu and Li (2021) explore the integration of EV charging stations into smart grids, emphasizing the role of advanced metering infrastructure in monitoring and managing load. Their empirical analysis shows that smart grids can effectively accommodate the growing demand for EV charging by enabling real-time communication between grid operators and charging stations.

This paper focuses on the large-scale integration of supercharging equipment in Shenzhen, is structured to provide a detailed analysis of the operational characteristics and impacts of this infrastructure on the city's energy landscape. The paper begins with an overview of the current state of new energy vehicle (NEV) adoption and the corresponding growth in charging infrastructure, highlighting the significant increase in NEV sales and the expansion of charging facilities. This sets the stage for a deeper exploration of the supercharging stations' distribution across various districts in Shenzhen and the timeline of their development.

The core of the paper is dedicated to analyzing the operational characteristics of supercharging equipment. This includes a clustering analysis of charging load characteristics from 20 typical supercharging stations, identifying four distinct types of load patterns: "Multiple Peaks in a Day," "Noon Peak," "Morning Valley and Evening Peak," and "Flat." The paper further examines how these load characteristics vary between weekdays and weekends, providing insights into the influence of user behavior and travel habits on charging demand. By identifying typical load patterns and their variations, the study offers valuable insights into optimizing the integration of supercharging facilities, which is crucial for maintaining grid stability and efficiency. The findings support the strategic planning and development of supercharging infrastructure, aligning with Shenzhen's goals to become a "Supercharging City" and contributing to the broader discourse on sustainable urban energy solutions.

2 Empirical Background in Shenzhen

In 2022, the sales of new energy vehicles (NEVs) in Shenzhen reached 239,000 units, a year-on-year increase of 22.3%, with a new car sales penetration rate of 61.8%. As of the end of June 2023, the total number of NEVs in the city reached 862,600, accounting for 21% of the total number of motor vehicles, with nearly 600,000 being new energy passenger cars.At the same time, the city's NEV charging infrastructure network continues to grow and improve. By the end of June 2023, more than 7,600 charging stations and over 190,000 charging facilities had been built, essentially establishing a city-wide charging infrastructure network. During the same period, 44 supercharging stations were built (according to research data as of November 2023), mainly distributed in areas such as Luohu, Futian, Nanshan, Bao'an, Longgang, Guangming, Pingshan, and Longhua.

Overall, since 2018, the sales of high-power charging models in China have continued to rise, showing a good development trend. According to the plans for supercharging models with a charging voltage of 800V and above released by major domestic car manufacturers, supercharging models began mass production in 2022, and high-end supercharging models meeting 3C (C is referred to as "charging rate") and above will be launched intensively in 2023. As supercharging technology continues to develop, mainstream models will generally support supercharging by 2025. According to publicly available market information, it is estimated that by 2025, there will be 43 models supporting supercharging technology (see Attachment 1). In line with the development and construction goals of the "Supercharging City," Shenzhen will continue to promote the construction of supercharging facilities throughout the "14th Five-Year Plan" period, with an expected 300 supercharging stations to be built, achieving a 1:1 ratio of supercharging to refueling facilities in the country, and initially establishing a supercharging city.

As of November 2023, Shenzhen has built a total of 44 supercharging stations. Among them, Nanshan District has 11 stations, Futian District and Bao'an District each have 9 stations, Longhua District has 6 stations, Guangming New District and Longgang District each have 3 stations, Pingshan District has 2 stations, and Luohu District has 1 station. In total, there are 76 planned supercharging piles. Among these supercharging stations, 32 were newly constructed and put into operation in 2023, with 1 station built and put into operation in 2021 and 11 stations in 2022.

3   Analysis of Typical Operating Characteristics of Current Supercharging Equipment

Based on supercharging stations that have been in operation for a long time with complete load data records, an analysis of their charging load characteristic curves, characteristic changes, and utilization levels of charging facilities is conducted. This helps identify the typical characteristics of supercharging facilities under different operating scenarios and supports further research on the impact of large-scale integration of supercharging equipment into the distribution network and the evaluation of efficiency and benefits.

3.1   Clustering Analysis of Charging Load Characteristics of Supercharging Stations

An in-depth analysis of the charging load characteristic data from 20 typical supercharging stations from January to October 2023 was conducted. Typical load characteristic curves were drawn, and statistical analysis methods were further used to perform clustering analysis on each curve. It was determined that the typical charging characteristics of the current supercharging equipment in Shenzhen can be divided into four types: "Multiple Peaks in a Day," "Noon Peak," "Morning Valley and Evening Peak," and "Flat."

a. "Multiple Peaks in a Day" Type

This type of charging load characteristic has a very typical "multiple peaks in a day" feature, with significant differences between peak and valley loads. This characteristic curve shows multiple charging load peaks throughout the day, with valley periods mainly concentrated around 10 a.m. and 3 p.m. It is speculated that the peak values of the curve are closely related to factors such as the travel habits of new energy vehicle users and charging costs (mainly electricity and service fees). Currently, this type of curve is the most common in the analysis results of supercharging station load characteristics in Shenzhen.

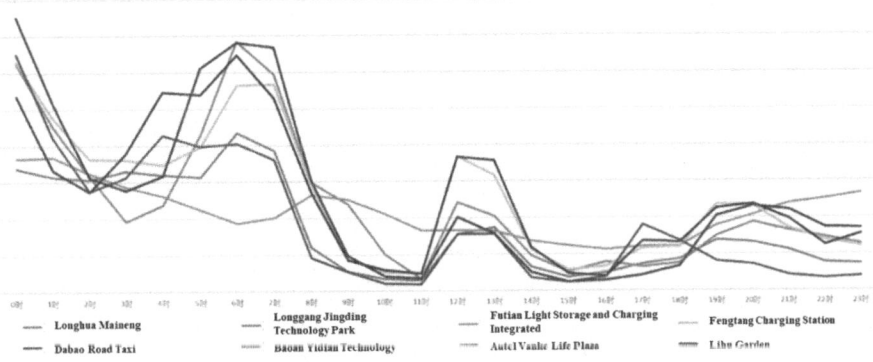

Fig. 1. "Multiple Peaks in a Day" Type Charging Load Characteristic Curve (Data Normalized)

b. "Noon Peak" Type

This type is characterized by a very prominent charging load peak occurring around noon (approximately 12 p.m.), while the rest of the day experiences relatively flat charging loads or primarily low load periods. This charging load characteristic is also quite common among the current supercharging stations.

c. "Morning Valley and Evening Peak" Type

The charging load valley occurs around 5 a.m., followed by a gradual increase in charging load, reaching a peak between 10 p.m. and midnight. The overall trend shows a gradual increase in charging load from morning to evening, without any significant low load periods during the day. This type is less influenced by factors such as travel habits and charging costs, and more reflects the characteristic of electric vehicle owners meeting their charging needs promptly. Currently, this type is less common.

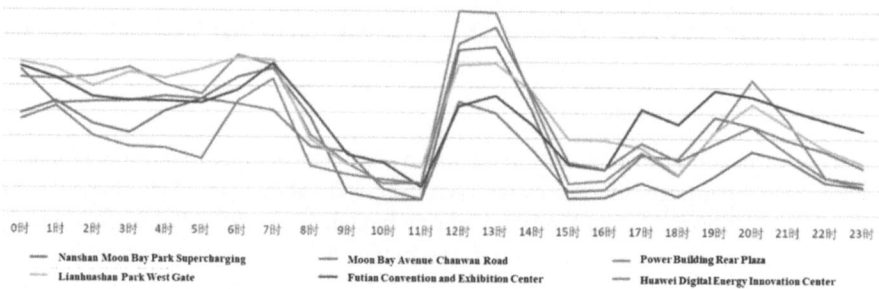

Fig. 2. "Noon Peak" Type Charging Load Characteristic Curve (Data Normalized)

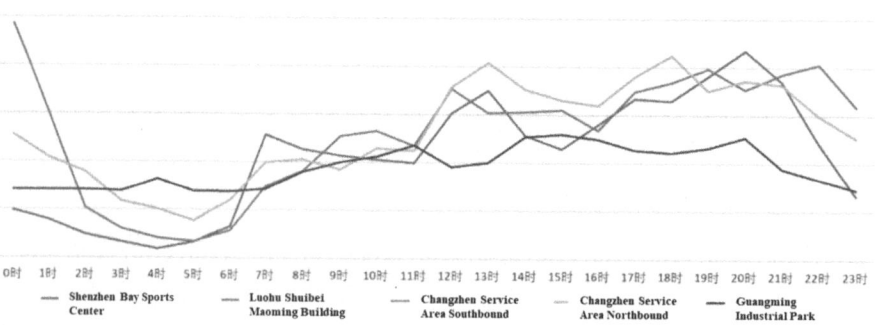

Fig. 3. "Morning Valley and Evening Peak" Type Charging Load Characteristic Curve (Data Normalized)

d. "Flat" Type

This type has weak peak and valley characteristics, with a smooth trend in charging load changes throughout the day, except for a low valley at midnight. There are no significant load fluctuations, and the overall curve is smooth. This characteristic is currently rare and is not expected to become mainstream.

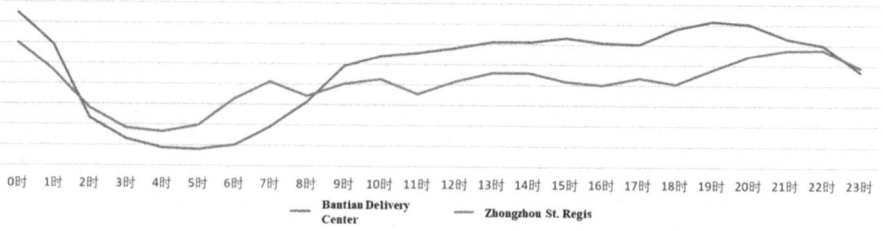

Fig. 4. "Flat" Type Charging Load Characteristic Curve (Data Normalized)

3.2 Analysis of Changes in Charging Load Characteristics of Supercharging Stations on Weekdays and Weekends

Due to changes in travel habits, the analysis determined that the load characteristics of typical supercharging stations in Shenzhen show the following changes on weekdays and weekends:

a At some supercharging stations, the peak charging load on weekends has changed significantly. For example, at the Nanshan Moon Bay Park and the Power Building Back Plaza supercharging stations, the trend and fluctuation of the load characteristic curve have not changed significantly, but the peak charging load has noticeably decreased.

b At some supercharging stations, the load characteristic curve has changed significantly. For instance, at the Shenzhen Bay Sports Center brand charging station, three peak periods appear on weekends at 10 a.m., 1 p.m., and 5 p.m. The newly added daytime charging peaks are significantly higher than the maximum charging load during the evening periods on weekdays.

c At some supercharging stations, while the characteristic curve and the scale of the charging load have not changed significantly, the timing of these events has shifted noticeably either forward or backward. For example, at the Jingding Technology Park and Lihu Garden charging stations, the overall trend of the characteristic curve in the morning on weekends has shifted nearly an hour later. Around 5 p.m., the charging characteristic curve that originally appeared during weekdays now appears about half an hour earlier. This indicates that the travel characteristics and charging behaviors of electric vehicle owners have changed somewhat during the weekend.

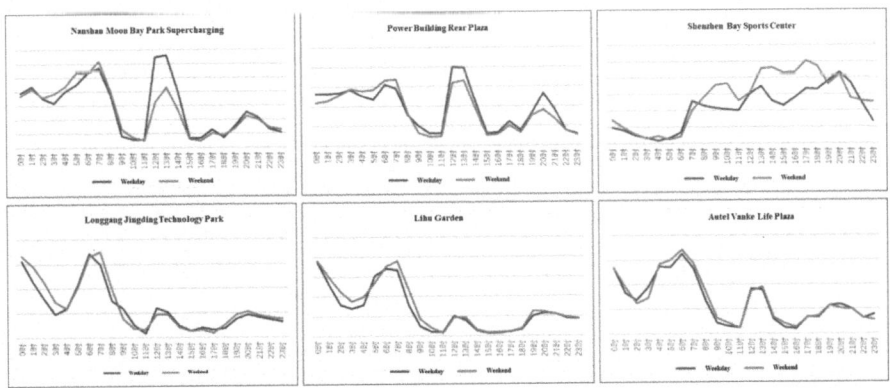

Fig. 5. Selected Load Characteristic Curves of Typical Supercharging Stations in Shenzhen on Weekdays and Weekends

3.3 Analysis of Changes in Charging Load Characteristics Before and After the Construction of Supercharging Facilities

Currently, many supercharging stations in Shenzhen are built by upgrading existing fast-charging stations. The changes in charging load characteristics before and after the upgrade are as follows:

a. Unchanged Characteristics, Shifted Timing: The load characteristic curve of the charging stations has not changed significantly before and after the upgrade, but the timing of peak and valley loads has shifted later. It is speculated that the supercharging method significantly shortens the charging time for some vehicle models, so owners do not need to arrive at the charging stations as early as they would with fast charging. As a result, the peak period for simultaneous vehicle charging at supercharging stations has shifted later.

b. Significant Improvement in Midnight Equipment Utilization Efficiency: Many supercharging stations have shown a significant increase in charging load during the midnight period. It is speculated that since supercharging equipment significantly shortens charging time, the impact on the owner's rest and operations is greatly reduced. Therefore, after comprehensive consideration, more owners choose the low-cost charging method after midnight.

c. Slight Reduction in Charging Load: Some charging stations have not experienced significant changes in their load characteristic curves, but the overall load level has slightly decreased. It is speculated that with the use of supercharging technology, the charging time is shortened, and although the charging power per vehicle has increased, the probability of multiple vehicles simultaneously undergoing high-power charging has decreased. Therefore, the overall load level of the charging station is slightly lower than before the upgrade.

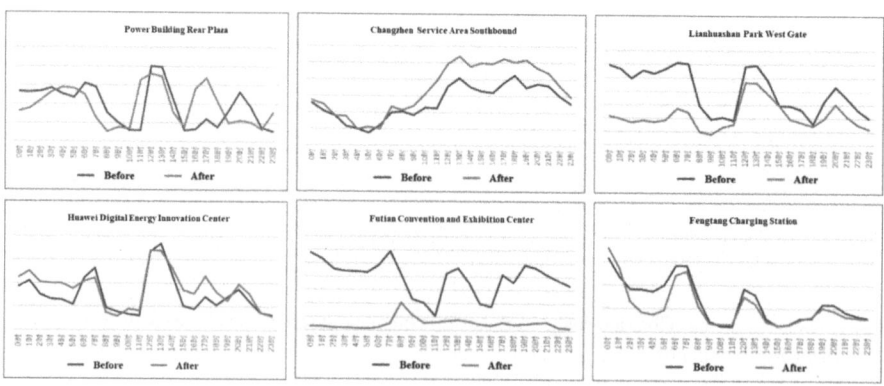

Fig. 6. Analysis of Changes in Load Characteristics Before and After the Upgrade of Typical Supercharging Stations (Data Normalized)

3.4 Annual Charging Load Characteristics Analysis of Supercharging Stations

Further analysis of the annual load characteristics of typical supercharging stations from January 1 to October 31, 2023, reveals the following features:

a. Rapid Growth in Charging Load: The overall trend shows a significant increase in the load at Shenzhen's supercharging stations. For example, by the end of October 2023, the total charging load at typical stations had reached approximately three times the level at the beginning of the year (with a maximum load of 16,377 kW occurring at 12:15 a.m. on September 28).

b. Close Association Between Load Fluctuations and Holidays: Observations indicate that significant charging peaks occur before or on holidays such as the Lantern Festival, Qingming Festival, Labor Day, Dragon Boat Festival, Mid-Autumn Festival, and National Day. In particular, 2023 featured an 8-day holiday for Mid-Autumn and National Day, with the highest charging load of the year occurring on September 28. Conversely, during the Spring Festival, when residents return home and travel, and production activities slow down, the charging load drops to the lowest level of the year.

c. Impact of Weather Conditions on Charging Behavior: Extreme monsoon weather in Shenzhen also leads to noticeable changes in charging load characteristics. For instance, during Typhoon Haikui on September 7 and 8, 2023, when heavy rain fell across the region, the charging load at supercharging stations significantly decreased, only to quickly return to normal levels after the rain subsided.

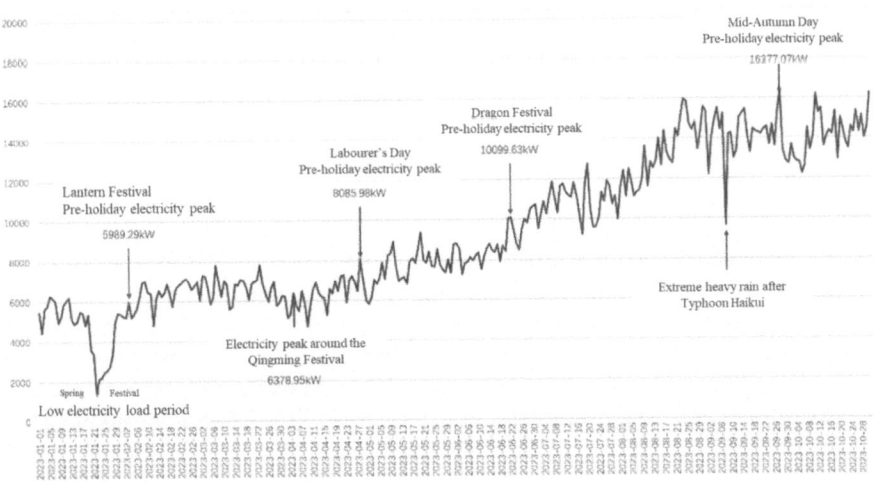

Fig. 7. Charging Load Characteristic Curve of Shenzhen's Supercharging Stations from January to October 2023

3.5 Analysis of the Operational Efficiency of Current Supercharging Stations

The operational efficiency of typical supercharging stations in Shenzhen is analyzed by observing two main indicators: load rate and transformer maximum load rate.

a. Load Rate: This is the percentage ratio of the average load to the maximum load during the statistical period and is an important indicator for measuring load variation and the utilization level of electrical equipment. The average load rate for 20 typical supercharging stations is 17.43%. Stations like Vanke Life Plaza and Bantian Delivery Center have load rates close to 30%, indicating high operational efficiency. In contrast, stations like Guangming Industrial Park and Dabao Road Taxi Terminal have load rates around 8%, suggesting room for improvement in overall operational efficiency.

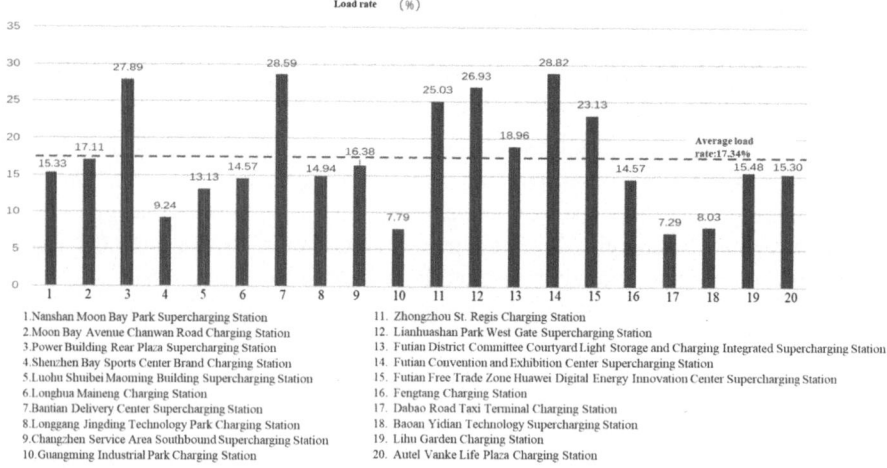

1. Nanshan Moon Bay Park Supercharging Station
2. Moon Bay Avenue Chanwan Road Charging Station
3. Power Building Rear Plaza Supercharging Station
4. Shenzhen Bay Sports Center Brand Charging Station
5. Luohu Shuibei Maoming Building Supercharging Station
6. Longhua Maineng Charging Station
7. Bantian Delivery Center Supercharging Station
8. Longgang Jingding Technology Park Charging Station
9. Changzhen Service Area Southbound Supercharging Station
10. Guangming Industrial Park Charging Station
11. Zhongzhou St. Regis Charging Station
12. Lianhuashan Park West Gate Supercharging Station
13. Futian District Committee Courtyard Light Storage and Charging Integrated Supercharging Station
14. Futian Convention and Exhibition Center Supercharging Station
15. Futian Free Trade Zone Huawei Digital Energy Innovation Center Supercharging Station
16. Fengtang Charging Station
17. Dabao Road Taxi Terminal Charging Station
18. Baoan Yidian Technology Supercharging Station
19. Lihu Garden Charging Station
20. Autel Vanke Life Plaza Charging Station

Fig. 8. Load Rate Level Statistics of Shenzhen's Current Supercharging Stations

b. Transformer Load Rate: Currently, only stations like Moon Bay Park and Jingding Technology Park have transformers operating within the economic range. Stations like the Futian District Committee Courtyard and Guangming Industrial Park have not fully utilized their transformer power supply capabilities. Stations like Chanwan Road and Futian Convention and Exhibition Center are advised to reasonably regulate charging loads to avoid prolonged transformer overload (Figs. 1, 2, 3, 4, 5, 6, 7, 8 and 9).

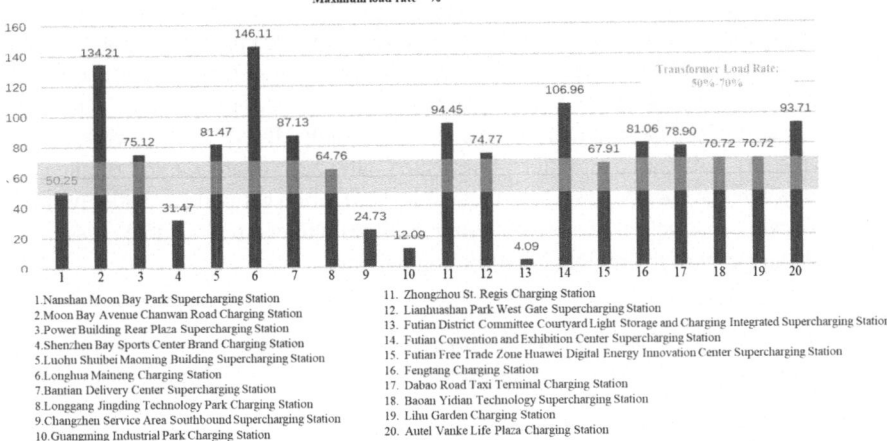

Fig. 9. Transformer Load Rate Level Statistics of Shenzhen's Current Supercharging Stations

4 Impact Analysis of Supercharging Equipment Integration into the Distribution Network

Based on the previous study of supercharging station load characteristics and the construction targets for supercharging stations in various districts outlined in the "Special Plan for New Energy Vehicle Supercharging Facilities in Shenzhen (2023–2025)," a comprehensive analysis of the impact of supercharging equipment integration into the distribution network is conducted. By overlaying the basic load of the distribution network in each district with the planned annual charging load of supercharging stations, the 8760-h load characteristic curve for each district's distribution network can be obtained. Further analysis of indicators such as peak-to-valley difference rate and annual load rate will help assess the impact of constructing 300 supercharging stations on the distribution networks in each district.

4.1 Impact Analysis of Supercharging Equipment Integration into the Distribution Network

During the analysis, it is assumed that the newly planned supercharging stations will adopt the same construction model as the existing ones, with both supercharging and fast-charging piles being built simultaneously. The load in each district is considered to grow at an average annual rate of 4.90%. The basic load of the distribution network is overlaid with the supercharging load characteristic curves for both weekdays and weekends.

As of March 2024, Shenzhen has planned to build a total of 300 supercharging stations. By then, the peak load of the entire distribution network is expected to increase by an additional 834.16 MW due to the charging load. The annual load rate of the city's distribution network is expected to slightly increase from 56.08% to 56.34%, a growth of 0.26%.

Overall, based on the current load characteristic curves of supercharging stations and user charging behavior patterns, the large-scale integration of supercharging stations has a very limited impact on the peak load of Shenzhen's power grid across all time domains (an increase of 834.16 MW, representing a 0.26% year-on-year growth). This indicates that the supply capacity and main load characteristics of the distribution network in most areas of the city will not be significantly affected. However, in areas like Longhua and Pingshan, where the basic load scale of the public distribution network is relatively small, the large-scale construction of supercharging facilities will exert noticeable pressure on the supply capacity of the regional distribution network.

4.2 Impact Analysis Considering Factors Such as Adaptation to Supercharging Technology and Vehicle Development

Currently, mid-to-high-end new energy vehicles (NEVs) that support supercharging technology account for approximately 20% of all NEV types. According to publicly available market information, it is expected that by 2025, the number of models supporting supercharging technology will increase to 43. This will make NEVs capable of using supercharging technology more common, and the utilization efficiency of supercharging stations is expected to further improve.

However, at the same time, private charging piles in residential communities and nearby slow-charging piles are also becoming more widespread. From the perspectives of charging convenience and cost, a significant proportion of private passenger car owners are more inclined to use slow-charging piles at their residences to replenish energy. In this scenario, the utilization efficiency of supercharging equipment may decrease compared to the current situation.

Considering these two influencing factors, two predictive scenarios for the charging load of supercharging stations in the planning year are proposed: a high scenario and a low scenario. In the high scenario, where the utilization efficiency of supercharging equipment increases, it is considered to be 1.2 times the current level. In the low scenario, where the utilization efficiency decreases, it is considered to be 0.8 times the current level. Considering the dual impact of the proliferation of vehicles compatible with supercharging technology and the development of private and slow-charging stations, the influence on the utilization efficiency of supercharging equipment is balanced between positive and negative aspects. Additionally, the construction of supporting power grids for supercharging stations must consider the hard boundary conditions such as the power of supercharging equipment. Therefore, it is recommended to use a middle-ground scenario as the primary reference for analyzing the impact of supercharging equipment integration on the load characteristics of the distribution network at this stage.

5 Summary of the Impact Analysis of Supercharging Station Integration into the Distribution Network

Based on the quantitative analysis conclusions above, the main impacts of integration are summarized as follows:

Firstly, Based on the actual operating patterns of existing supercharging stations and their impact on the overall load characteristics of district distribution networks, the construction of 300 supercharging stations as per the planning target and their integration into the distribution network will not significantly affect the supply capacity and main load characteristics of most areas in the city. However, in areas like Longhua and Pingshan, where the basic load scale of the public distribution network is relatively small, large-scale construction of supercharging facilities will exert noticeable pressure on the supply capacity of the regional distribution network.

Secondly, after a period of operation, typical existing supercharging stations have released their charging service capacity. Observational analysis of their load characteristics and impact after integration into the distribution network shows that most supercharging stations have higher utilization efficiency at night. This characteristic can, to some extent, improve the equipment utilization efficiency and overall load rate level of the regional distribution network. However, since the charging load itself is relatively small, the improvement effect is not significant.

Thirdly, to meet the demand for fast charging, supercharging equipment generally has a high rated power. This means that the supporting power grid needs to provide more ample supply capacity to meet its integration needs. However, compared to fast and slow charging equipment, in a scenario where the total city-wide charging demand is fixed, supercharging equipment requires a larger scale of supporting power grid construction but has lower utilization efficiency (due to shorter charging times per vehicle). Therefore, for power grid companies, the construction of supercharging stations has a more pronounced impact on the operational efficiency and benefits of the distribution network. It is recommended to communicate fully with the government and relevant units on such matters to obtain policy and financial support as much as possible.

The construction and market application of supercharging equipment are still in the early stages. The construction model, operation method, load characteristics, as well as the battery technology of new energy vehicles and the charging behavior habits of car owners, may change in the future. The analysis, demonstration, and quantitative evaluation research involved in this document are based on the existing typical supercharging stations. Therefore, if relevant boundary conditions are adjusted in the future, the conclusions proposed in this study will need to be adjusted and improved after further investigation and supplementation.

Acknowledgement. The authors gratefully acknowledge the editor and the reviewers' comments and helpful suggestions. This research is supported in part by the Guangdong Provincial Department of Education's General University Characteristic Innovation Project (2022WTSCX265), the Shenzhen Philosophy and Social Science Co-construction Project (SZ2022D038), the Shenzhen Polytechnic University Research Start-up Project (6022312019K), and the Shenzhen Polytechnic University Social Science Youth Innovation Project (6022310013S).

References

1. Zhang, Y., Wang, C.: Impact of electric vehicle charging on power grid load and solutions. J. Power. Sources **450**, 227667 (2020)
2. Li, J., Chen, H.: Analysis of electric vehicle charging station distribution and its impact on urban power grids. Energy Rep. **5**, 1115–1123 (2019)
3. Wang, X., Liu, Z.: Optimization of charging infrastructure for electric vehicles: a review. Renew. Sustain. Energy Rev. **145**, 111081 (2021)
4. Zhao, L., Sun, Y.: The role of fast charging stations in urban electric vehicle adoption. Transp. Res. Part D: Transp. Environ. **85**, 102390 (2020)
5. Chen, M., Zhang, T.: Electric vehicle charging infrastructure planning: a review of models and methods. Renew. Sustain. Energy Rev. **82**, 1927–1940 (2018)
6. Liu, Y., Gao, J.: The impact of electric vehicle charging on power grid stability. J. Clean. Prod. **215**, 444–456 (2019)
7. Xu, Q., Li, S.: Strategies for integrating electric vehicle charging stations into smart grids. Energy **219**, 119555 (2021)
8. Huang, R., Wang, J.: Assessing the impact of electric vehicle charging on distribution networks. Appl. Energy **262**, 114553 (2020)
9. Feng, S., Yang, X.: Electric vehicle charging infrastructure and its impact on power grid load. Energy Procedia **158**, 4363–4368 (2019)
10. Zhang, L., Zhou, P.: The development of electric vehicle charging infrastructure in china: challenges and opportunities. Energy Policy **149**, 112023 (2021)
11. Wang, H., Li, Y.: Electric vehicle charging demand and its impact on power grid load. J. Energy Storage **32**, 101859 (2020)
12. Chen, X., Liu, H.: The role of electric vehicle charging stations in urban energy systems. Energy Convers. Manage. **171**, 133–142 (2018)
13. Zhao, Y., Zhang, Q.: Electric vehicle charging infrastructure: a review of current development and future perspectives. Renew. Sustain. Energy Rev. **113**, 109254 (2019)
14. Li, F., Wang, Z.: The impact of electric vehicle charging on power grid load and solutions. Energy Rep. **6**, 1115–1123 (2020)
15. Sun, J., Chen, L.: Electric vehicle charging infrastructure and its impact on power grid load. Energy Procedia **158**, 4363–4368 (2021)

Secure Similar Adjacent Vertex Query on Sparse Graph Data in Cloud Environment

Yun Tian[1], Bin Wu[1,2(✉)], Jiaoli Shi[1,2], Caicai Zhang[3], and Du Xu[1]

[1] School of Computer and Big Data Science, Jiujiang University,
Jiujiang 332005, China
wubincs@gmail.com
[2] Jiujiang Key Laboratory of Network and Information Security,
Jiujiang 332005, China
[3] School of Modern Information Technology, Zhejiang Polytechnic University
of Mechanical and Electrical Engineering, Hangzhou 310053, China

Abstract. The development of cloud computing and the widespread application of cloud services have made outsourcing services more convenient. The need for individuals and businesses to store and manipulate the graph data they generate is growing rapidly. The unreliability and insecurity of cloud servers make outsourcing graph data a great risk of information leakage. To effectively protect data security, encrypting outsourced data is a useful method. The adjacent vertex query is a very commonly used and fundamental operation, and similarity search is a widely used and powerful tool to improve the scope and functionality of queries. After outsourcing encrypted sparse graph data to cloud servers, it becomes very inconvenient to use and manipulate the data. In this work, we present a scheme to realize the adjacent vertex query supporting similarity search on sparse graph data in cloud environment (SSAQ), which also protects the security of the information. This work uses edit distance and the searchable encryption principle to construct query index, and next implement the similar adjacent vertex query on cloud server. This work provides a formal security analysis, and also gives the experimental comparison and analysis.

Keywords: adjacent vertex query · graph data · searchable encryption · cloud environment

1 Introduction

The development of cloud computing is advancing rapidly, and it makes outsourcing services more convenient [1]. The sparse graph data is widely used in industrial, production, and scientific research fields, and the generated graph data is growing rapidly. The security of the graph data outsourced to cloud servers needs to be fully considered [2]. To ensure the security of outsourced graph data, these data need to be encrypted before outsourcing to the cloud

© The Author(s), under exclusive license to Springer Nature Switzerland AG 2025
J. Zeng and L.-J. Zhang (Eds.): EDGE 2024, LNCS 15424, pp. 95–104, 2025.
https://doi.org/10.1007/978-3-031-77069-2_8

platform [3]. As these graph data outsourced to cloud servers is encrypted, accessing and querying these data is a very challenging problem.

The adjacent vertex query is a very useful operation in sparse graph data, and it is also a fundamental prerequisite for other operations and processing [4,5]. The subgraph query, community detection and pattern matching are all realized based upon the adjacent vertex query [6–8]. The adjacent vertex query with similarity search improve usability and the user's search experience.This work uses the edit distance and searchable encryption principle to realize the secure similar adjacent vertex query on the graph data in cloud environment.

If all the outsourced graph data is downloaded and queried locally, it is very uneconomical. Therefore, implementing similar adjacent vertex query directly on the cloud server side can be very beneficial and challenging [9,10]. The searchable encryption is a useful technique in some studies [11–15], and is currently an important and popular research branch [16–18]. Now the issue of secure queries on outsourced graph data is also an important research direction, and some achievements continue to emerge [19–22]. Due to the complexity of graph data relationships, these research methods cannot solve the problem of the similar adjacent vertex query on the graph data in cloud environment.

To solve this problem, we present a scheme to realize the secure similar adjacent vertex query on sparse graph data in cloud environment (SSAQ). The SSAQ scheme can realize similar adjacent vertex query by an index and query tokens on cloud servers. We first build the query index according to the searchable encryption principle and the edit distance, we next send the index and encrypted graph data to cloud servers. The cloud servers achieve the similar adjacent vertex query by the secure index and the query tokens, and returns the query results to query user. The security proof and the experimental analysis demonstrate that our scheme is secure and effective. The contribution of this work is summarized as follows.

(1) We present a scheme to settle the problem of secure similar adjacent vertex query on encrypted graph.
(2) We prove that our scheme is of security by the security analysis.
(3) The experimental results indicate the effectiveness of our scheme.

The rest of the work is organized as follows. Section 2 introduces the preliminaries of this work. Section 3 designs the construction of the scheme. Section 4 and Sect. 5 evaluate our scheme both from security and experiments. Section 6 introduces the related work. Finally, Sect. 7 concludes the paper.

2 Preliminaries

In this work, we use $a \leftarrow A$ to represent that an element a is selected from set A, and $a \xleftarrow{R} A$ to denote that an element a is selected from set A uniformly and randomly [14,23]. We use $\|$ to to represent string concatenation [14]. The main notations used in the work are listed in Table 1.

To implement the similarity search, we adopt the edit distance which is a commonly used technique in information retrieval [24], and we use the edit

Table 1. Summary of notations

Notations	Denotations
G	A sparse graph data set
I	A query index
V	A set of all vertices of the graph G
$|V|$	The number of vertices of the graph G
H_i	A set of all adjacency vertices of similarity keywords set for vertex v_i $v_i(1 \leq i \leq |V|)$
m	The maximum number of adjacent vertex of similarity keywords
Q_{h_i}	A set of encrypted query tokens of element $h_i(1 \leq i \leq m)$
R_{h_i}	A set of query results of element $h_i(1 \leq i \leq m)$
$Enc_{key}(\cdot)$	A semantic security symmetric encryption function used in our scheme
$Dec_{key}(\cdot)$	A semantic security symmetric decryption function used in our scheme

distance as a similarity measure to process graph vertices. We also use a suppressing technique to construct an effective set of similarity keywords from the set of graph vertices. Based on this, we construct a secure index for executing queries on cloud servers.

3   Scheme Construction

3.1   Scheme Overview

In the cloud outsourcing environment, the system model of our scheme illustrated in Fig. 1 mainly contains different entities: the cloud server, the data owner, and the user. The cloud server is responsible for storing, computing, and processing the outsourced graph data and query index of the data owner. When a user has a need for the data, the cloud server implements these operations by using secure indexes and query tokens. In the construction process of the index and our scheme, we use the searchable encryption idea to implement it, and we assume that the query user has the authorization key to obtain the query request [14]. We decide to use an adaptive attack model for cloud servers in this work [14,16].

In the scheme of this work, the core task is to build the secure index and query tokens, and how to implement the similar adjacent vertex query. The main steps of this scheme include secret key generation, secure index construction and the implementation of adjacent vertex query.

3.2   Scheme Designing

We now construct our SSAQ scheme. Following the previous searchable encryption schemes [14,16], the query solution we construct can achieve adjacent vertex query with similarity searchover on encrypted graph in cloud environment.

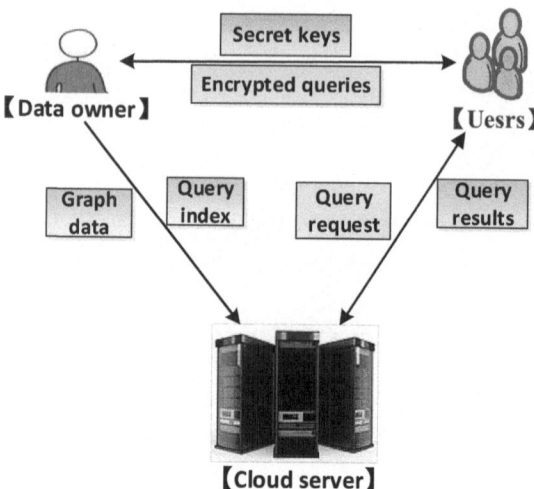

Fig. 1. Query system model on encrypted graph in cloud environment

The vertex set of the sparse graph is represented as $V = \{v_1, \ldots, v_n\}$. To implement the similarity search, we adopt the edit distance to construct a set of similar keywords for graph vertices [16]. For a graph vertex v_i and similarity threshold d, we construct its similarity keyword set $S_{v_i,d}$. For any element v_i' of the set $S_{v_i,d}$, The *edit distance* $ed(v_i, v') \leq d$. As the size of the generated set is too large, the suppressing technique is used in this work to reduce the size of similar sets. That is to say, we use a wildcard " $*$ " at any position to represent the three operations of character insertion, deletion, and replacement. Based on the new set $S_{v_i,d}$, we construct a set of their adjacent vertex H_i. To protect their security, the elements in the set are encrypted. All sets of adjacent vertex are represented as H.

To achieve the similar adjacent vertex query on encrypted graph in cloud environment, we construct a query index based on the constructing adjacent vertex set. For a vertex $v_i (1 \leq i \leq |V|)$ in set V, the corresponding set of adjacent vertices is H_i, and the number of elements in the set is represented as $|H_i|$. For $1 \leq j \leq |H_i|$, we build a label for h_t by concatenating h_t with j ($h_t \in H_i$, $1 \leq t \leq |H_i|$), and the label is denoted as $h_t||j$. Then all labels related to h_t are represented as $L_{h_t} = (h_t||1, \ldots, h_t|||H_i|)$. The matching adjacent vertex contents of each element in set L_{h_t} are stored in the query index. When carrying out adjacent vertex query, it is equivalent to querying the matching elements in the index through all the labels in the set L_{h_t}. Each label corresponds to only one element in the index. To protect information leakage, the number of adjacent verte is the same by adding some perturbing values to the query index.

When the query index is built, the graph data and the query index are outsourced to the cloud platform. When the adjacent vertex query is executed, the query token used for conducting adjacent vertex query is constructed by the data owner, that is, $Q_{h_t} = (q_{t1}, \ldots, q_{tm}) = (Enc_{s_i}(h_t||1), \ldots, Enc_{s_i}(h_t||m))$.

KeysGen(l): //*Generating secret keys.*

Generate random keys k_i, $s_i \xleftarrow{R} (0,1)^l$, where, $1 \leq i \leq m$.

BuildingArray(G, k_i): //*Building adjacent vertex array.*

1. The vertexs set in sparse graph G is $V = (v_1, \ldots, v_n)$.
2. The similarity keywords set of v_i is $S_{vi,d}$ after similarity editing and generation.
3. Building an array H_i for the element of $S_{vi,d}$, and each entry in the array represents an an adjacent vertex. All sets of adjacent vertex are represented as $H = (H_1, \ldots, H_n)$.
4. For the array H_i $(1 \leq i \leq |H_i|)$:

    For $1 \leq j \leq |H_i|$:

    Set $h_{ij} = <Enc_{s_i} (adjvalue) >$, and set $H_i[j] = h_{ij}$. //*adjvalue is vertex information.*

    The element is encrypted, and get the encrypted array H_i .

BuildingIndex(G, s_i): //*Building query index.*

1. For each element h_{ij} in the array H_i, where, $1 \leq i, j \leq |H_i|$,

    (1) Compute $position = Enc_{s_i} (h_{ij} \| j)$;

    (2) Set $I[position] = H_i[j]$.

2. For the array H_i, if $|H_i| < m$, then set $(m - |H_i|)$ values in I, and there are m adjacency vertex in I for each $h_{ij} \in H_i$. This can be done as follows:

    (1) Let $u = |H_i|$ be the number of elements in I that already contains h_{ij} ;

    (2) For $1 \leq c \leq m-u$, compute $position = Enc_{s_i}(0^t \|(m + c))$, set $I[position] = Enc_{s_i}(0 \|(|H_i| + c) \| 0^r)$.

ConstructingToken(h_i, s_i):

$Q_{h_i} = (q_{i1}, \ldots, q_{im}) = (Enc_{s_i}(h_i \| 1), \ldots, Enc_{s_i}(h_i \| m))$.

ExecutingQuery(I, Q_{h_i}):

1. For $1 \leq j \leq m$, if $I(q_{ij})$ exists, then $I(q_{ij})$ is added to the result set R_{h_i} .
2. Output the result set R_{h_i} .

Fig. 2. Ajacent vertex query scheme constructing process

When a query is executed, the cloud server processes it through this query token and the query index, and then feeds the results of the query back to the user.

In this work, we make use of l and r to represent the security parameters used in our scheme. The constructing process of the scheme about the ajacent vertex query with similarity search is described in Fig. 2.

4   Security Analysis

We are now provide a security analysis of our proposed scheme. The scheme follows searchable symmetric encryption mechanism of the literature [12,14,16]. When executing a query, the cloud server cannot obtain the graph data information and user's privacy. In this work, we prove the ajacent vertex query scheme satisfies the adaptive semantic security, and an adversary cannot distinguish the views of the two histories [14]. The cloud server cannot learn the additional information beyond the contents about the trace, and thus our SSAQ scheme is secure. The security theorem for our similar adjacent vertex query scheme is stated below.

Theorem 1. Our SSAQ scheme meets the adaptive semantic security.

Proof. To prove the semantic security, we describe a polynomial size simulator S. For all $q \in N$, S can generate a view $(V_q^t)^*$ such that $(V_q^t)^*$ is indistinguishable from $V_K^t(H_q)$ of the adversary, where K is a key, and $0 \leq t \leq q$.

For $t = 0$, the simulator S constructs the simulated index I^* on the partial history $T_r(H_q^0)$ to simulate the index I, both of which are equally large in scale. It is obvious that I^* is indistinguishable from I. Otherwise, the outputs of a symmetric encryption function and the random strings of the same size are distinguishable. Thus, $(V_q^0)^*$ is indistinguishable from $V_K^0(H_q)$.

For $1 \leq t \leq q$, the simulator S will build the query tokens $(Q_1^*, \ldots, Q_t^*)$ included in $(V_q^t)^*$. When constructing these tokens, S can reuse the tokens $(Q_1^*, \ldots, Q_{t-1}^*)$ that were included in $(V_q^{t-1})^*$. Alternatively, the simulator could reconstruct these query tokens from $T_r(H_q^{t-1})$.

To build Q_t^*, for any $1 \leq j \leq t - 1$, the simulator S first checks whether H_q^{t-1} contains h_t by checking if its search pattern equals to 1. If it is not 1, the simulator S makes use of the contents $T_r(H_q^t)$ about R_{h_t}, that is, $L_{h_t} = (h_t||1, \ldots, h_t||m)$. The simulator randomly selects an address from I^* for $1 \leq i \leq m$, insuring that all a_i are pairwise different, and builds the query information $Q_t^* = (a_1, \ldots, a_m)$. Otherwise, if H_q^{t-1} contains h_t, then the simulator S retrieves the query information associated with h_t and assigns it to Q_t^*. It ensures that if H_q^t contains repeated query tokens, then the query tokens included in $(V_q^t)^*$ are the same.

It is obvious that, the query tokens $(Q_1^*, \ldots, Q_t^*)$ in $(V_q^t)^*$ is indistinguishable from the query tokens $(Q_1, \ldots, Q_t)$ in $V_K^t(H_q)$, otherwise, the outputs of a symmetric encryption algorithm and the random strings of the same size are distinguishable. So, for $0 \leq t \leq q$, there is no polynomial size adversary could distinguish between $(V_q^t)^*$ and $V_K^t(H_q)$. Therefore, the SSAQ theorem has been proven to be of security.

5 Experimental Evaluations

In this section, We carry out the experimental analysis for the scheme on the Enron email network graph [25,26]. We complete the experiment by C programming language over both local working computer and cloud server. The local computer runs Win10 and has an Intel Core 6 CPU running at 3.5 GHz, and 8GB of RAM. The cloud server runs Linux and is equipped with 10 CPU cores and 16GB of RAM.

The analysis and evaluation of query performance in this scheme is performed by means of query index and query token, and the ajacent vertex query is executed on the cloud server. We compare and analyze the performance and efficiency of ajacent vertex query through two scenarios. One is to use the maximum number of degrees of vertices in extreme cases (shorter form MDE), and the other is used in our SSAQ scheme.

In the ajacent vertex query operations, the cloud server completes the query operation with a secure index based on the user's requirements. Figure 3 gives the query performance results, where the Y-axis represents the query time, and the X-axis represents the number of vertices or edges in the graph data.

As can be seen in Fig. 3, the query time is approximately linear to the number of vertices or edges in the graph. The experimental results show that our scheme has better query effectiveness. Although some operations need to be performed locally, such as building indexes, and this takes up some overhead, it is well worth the query functionality implemented.

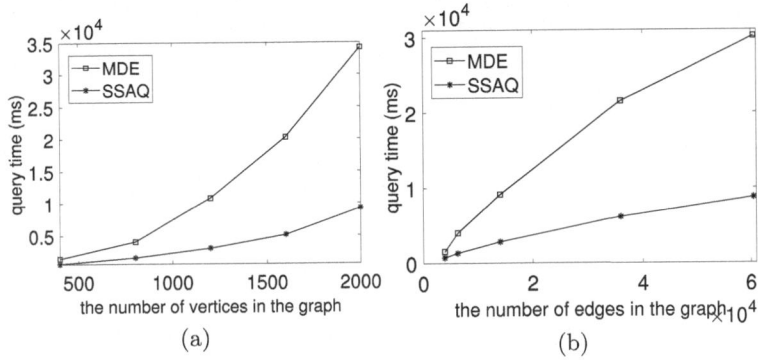

Fig. 3. Query execution time

In short, from the experimental results, the time overhead of the query scheme changes approximately linearly with the number of vertices or edges in the graph. The total cost of the experiment is acceptable and the scheme accomplishes the similar adjacent vertex query. The cloud server cannot know the contents of the index and query results, and our scheme meet availability and effectiveness.

6   Related Work

The processing and application of outsourced data are often used in cloud computing. The searchable encryption has a great role and value in cloud outsourcing, and there are usually two outsourcing encryption processing methods. They are symmetric searchable encryption method and asymmetric encryption method [14,15]. As the symmetric encryption is more efficient than the asymmetrical encryption, we adopt the symmetric encryption in this work.

Song et al. firstly proposed the designing thought of searchable symmetric encryption by using the stream cipher [11]. Goh proposed the concept of secure index, and used the bloom filter to construct an index for each file for the first time [13]. Based on previous research, Curtmola et al. proposed two symmetric search encryption schemes, namely, non-adaptive scheme and adaptive scheme. Boneh et al. first proposed a searchable encryption scheme based on public key algorithm [15]. In the following period, some researchers gradually proposed some extended searchable encryption methods [16–18], and these methods improve the efficiency of the query and expand the search function. However, these existing methods cannot implement the ajacent vertex query with similarity search on encrypted graph.

Recently, the problem of secure queries on outsourced graph has aroused extensive research, and some research results have emerged [19–22]. Chase et al. proposed the thought of structure encryption and implemented encrypted queries for any structured data [19]. Cao et al. were the first to address and implement the subgraph query problem [20]. Shen et al. achieved a constrained shortest path query scheme over encrypted graph data and proposed a tree-based ciphertext comparison protocol [21]. Ciucanu et al. proposed and achieved a scheme to perform SPARQL evaluation-enabled secure queries on encrypted graph [22]. But these methods cannot solve our problem of ajacent vertex query supporting similarity search.

7 Conclusion

In this work, we present a new scheme to implement similar adjacent vertex query on encrypted graph in cloud environment. For achieving the similar adjacent vertex query, we adopt searchable symmetric encryption mechanism and edit distance algorithm to build secure index and query scheme. We provid the security proof for the proposed scheme and demonstrate its effectiveness through experimental analysis.

In the future work, we will integrate the query of outsourced graph with big data technology to improve the efficiency of operation. We will also consider the operation and processing of outsourced dynamic graph data in big data scenarios.

Acknowledgment. The authors gratefully acknowledge the editor and the reviewers' comments and helpful suggestions. This research is supported in part by the National Nature Science Foundation of China (No. 62262033 and 62062045), the Visiting Engineer Cooperation Project of Zhejiang Province (No. FG2023061).

References

1. Jiang, J., Wang, D., Zhang, G., et al.: QPause: quantum-resistant password-protected data outsourcing for cloud storage. IEEE Trans. Serv. Comput. **17**(3), 1140–1153 (2024)
2. Liu, Q., Peng, Y., Jiang, H., et al.: Authorized keyword search on mobile devices in secure data outsourcing. IEEE Trans. Mob. Comput. **23**(5), 4181–4195 (2024)
3. Zhou, Z., Wan, Y., Cui, Q., et al.: Blockchain-based secure and efficient secret image sharing with outsourcing computation in wireless networks. IEEE Trans. Wireless Commun. **23**(1), 423–435 (2024)
4. Liu, W., Wen, D., Wang, H., et al.: Skyline nearest neighbor search on multi-layer graphs. In: 2014 IEEE 35th International Conference on Data Engineering Workshops, IEEE: Piscataway, N.J., USA, 2019, pp. 259–265 (2019)

5. Potamias, M., Bonchi, F., Gionis, A., Kollios, G., et al.: K-nearest neighbors in uncertain graphs. Proc. VLDB Endowment **3**(1), 997–1008 (2010)
6. Wang, R., Yan, J., Yang, X., et al.: Combinatorial learning of robust deep graph matching: an embedding based approach. IEEE Trans. Pattern Anal. Mach. Intell. **45**(6), 6984–7000 (2023)
7. Bazgan, C., Pontoizeau, T., Tuza, Z., et al.: Finding a potential community in networks. Theoret. Comput. Sci. **769**, 32–42 (2019)
8. Ferrer-Cid, P., Barceló-Ordinas, J., García-Vidal, J., et al.: Volterra graph-based outlier detection for air pollution sensor networks. IEEE Trans. Netw. Sci. Eng. **9**(4), 2759–2771 (2023)
9. Li, X., Ye, H., Li, T., et al.: Efficient and secure outsourcing of differentially private data publishing with multiple evaluators. IEEE Trans. Dependable Secure Comput. **19**(1), 67–76 (2022)
10. Zhang, X., Zhao, J., Xu, C., et al.: DOPIV: post-quantum secure identity-based data outsourcing with public integrity verification in cloud storage. IEEE Trans. Serv. Comput. **15**(1), 334–345 (2022)
11. Song, D.X., Wagner, D., Perrig, A.: Practical techniques for searches on encrypted data. In: Proceeding 2000 IEEE Symposium on Security and Privacy (S&P'00), IEEE: Los Alamitos, CA, USA, 2000; pp. 44–55 (2000)
12. Chang, Y.C., Howser, G., Mitzenmacher, M., Madria, S.: Privacy preserving keyword searches on remote encrypted data. In: Third International Conference, Applied Cryptography and Network Security (ACNS'05), pp. 442–455. Springer: Berlin, Germany (2005). https://doi.org/10.1007/11496137_30
13. Goh, E.J.: Secure indexes. In: Cryptology ePrint Archive, Report 2003/216 (2003)
14. Curtmola, R., Garay, J., Kamara, S., Ostrovsky, R.: Searchable symmetric encryption: improved definitions and efficient constructions. In: Proceedings of the 13th ACM Conference on Computer and Communications Security (ccs'06), pp. 79–88. ACM: Alexandria, VA, United states (2006)
15. Boneh, D., Crescenzo, G.D., Ostrovsky, R., Persiano, G.: Public key encryption with keyword search revisited. In: International Conference on Computational Science and Its Applications (ICCSA'08), pp. 1249–1259. Springer: Berlin, Germany (2008). https://doi.org/10.1007/978-3-540-69839-5_96
16. Wang, C., Ren, K., Yu, S., et al.: Achieving usable and privacy-assured similarity search over outsourced cloud data. In: Proceedings of the IEEE INFOCOM 2012, pp. 451–459. IEEE: Orlando, FL, USA (2012)
17. Mei, Z., Yu, J., Zhang, C., et al.: Secure multi-dimensional data retrieval with access control and range query in the cloud. Inf. Syst. **122**, 102343 (2024)
18. Oyamada, R.S., Shimomura, L.C., Barbon, S., et al.: A meta-learning configuration framework for graph-based similarity search indexes. Inf. Syst. **112**, 102123 (2023)
19. Chase, M., Kamara, S., et al.: Structured encryption and controlled disclosure. Structured encryption and controlled disclosure. In: Cryptology and Information Security 2010, pp. 577–594 (2010)
20. Cao, N., Yang, Z., Wang, C., Ren, K., Lou, W.: Privacy-preserving query over encrypted graph-structured data in cloud computing. In: Proceedings of the 2011 31st International Conference on Distributed Computing Systems (ICDCS'11), IEEE: Los Alamitos, CA, USA, (2011), pp. 393–402 (2011)
21. Shen, M., Ma, B., Zhu, L., et al.: Cloud-based approximate constrained shortest distance queries over encrypted graphs with privacy protection. IEEE Trans. Inf. Forensics Secur. **13**, 940–953 (2018)

22. Ciucanu, R., Lafourcade, P., et al.: GOOSE: a secure framework for graph outsourcing and SPARQL evaluation. In: Proceedings of Data and Applications Security
and Privacy - 34th Annual IFIP WG 11.3 Conference (DBSec 2020), pp. 347–366.
Springer: Regensburg, Germany (2020). https://doi.org/10.1007/978-3-030-49669-
2_20

23. Katz, J., Lindell, Y.: Introduction to Modern Cryptography. Chapman &
Hall/CRC (2007)

24. Singhal, A.: Modern information retrieval: a brief overview. Bull. IEEE Comput.
Soc. Tech. Committee Data Eng. **24**(4), 35–43 (2001)

25. Leskovec, J., Lang, K.J., Dasgupta, A., et al.: Community structure in large networks: natural cluster sizes and the absence of large well-defined clusters. Internet
Math. **6**(1), 29–123 (2009)

26. Klimt, B., Yang, Y.: Introducing the Enron corpus. In: First Conference on Email
and Anti-Spam (CEAS'04), pp. 1–2. Google, Microsoft, etc.: Mountain View, CA,
USA (2004)

Author Index